# CONTENTS

Introduction
Chapter 1: Improving Productivity
Chapter 2: The "I Don't Know" Mindset
Chapter 3: The "Already Told You" Tactic
Chapter 4: Feigning Ignorance
Chapter 5: The "My Job is Done" Approach
Chapter 6: Countering by Asking
Chapter 7: Selective Hearing
Chapter 8: Keeping Things Vocal
Chapter 9: Saying You Understand
Chapter 10: The Power of Assumptions
Chapter 11: Strategic Silence
Chapter 12: The Call Strategy
Chapter 13: Testing Market Reactions
Chapter 14: Hidden Responsibilities
Chapter 15: Using Higher Authority
Chapter 16: Generic Agreements
Chapter 17: Passing Responsibility
Chapter 18: New Boss Dynamics
Chapter 19: Saying No
Chapter 20: Teamwork Rhetoric
Chapter 21: Minimal Email Communication
Chapter 22: Misleading Through Silence
Chapter 23: Agreement by Call
Chapter 24: Assigning Unrelated Tasks
Chapter 25: Sales Dynamics
Chapter 26: Constraints Management

Chapter 27: Adaptive Communication
Chapter 28: Family-Run Businesses
Conclusion

# INTRODUCTION

**1. Overview: The Landscape of Bad Bosses and Colleague**

In every workplace, you're bound to encounter a variety of personalities, each with their unique approach to managing tasks, responsibilities, and interactions. Among these, bad bosses and challenging colleagues stand out as significant hurdles to productivity and morale. They employ a range of tactics to manipulate, delegate, and often sidestep their responsibilities. Understanding these behaviors is crucial to navigating your career successfully and maintaining a healthy work environment.

This book aims to shed light on the different types of problematic bosses and colleagues you might meet throughout your professional journey. From those who constantly shift their workload to others, to those who feign ignorance to avoid tasks, these individuals can create a toxic atmosphere that hampers team dynamics and personal growth. By recognizing and understanding these tactics, you can equip yourself with the tools needed to handle these challenges effectively.

**2. Purpose: Navigating Workplace Tactics**

The primary purpose of this book is to provide insights into various workplace tactics used by difficult bosses and colleagues. It's not just about identifying these behaviors but also about developing strategies to counteract them. Whether you're dealing with a manager who never takes responsibility, a coworker who always seems to evade tasks, or a team member who manipulates situations to their advantage, this book offers practical advice on how to manage these interactions.

By the end of this book, you will have a deeper understanding of the underlying motives behind these tactics and the skills to navigate them. This knowledge will empower you to maintain your integrity, protect your workload, and foster a more collaborative and respectful work environment.

## 3. Scope: What You Will Learn

Throughout the chapters, you will explore a variety of common tactics used by bad bosses and colleagues, including:

- Improving Productivity: Techniques used to offload work onto others under the guise of boosting overall productivity.
- The "I Don't Know" Mindset: How claiming ignorance can be a tool to avoid responsibilities.
- The "Already Told You" Tactic: Minimalistic communication strategies that leave others in the dark.
- Feigning Ignorance: Using confusion as a means to delegate tasks back to others.
- "My Job is Done" Approach: Quick, incomplete task execution followed by passing the buck for corrections.
- Countering by Asking: Deflecting questions by making the requestor think and provide answers.
- Selective Hearing: Ignoring unbeneficial comments to maintain control over discussions.
- Keeping Things Vocal: Relying on verbal agreements to avoid accountability.
- The Power of Assumptions: Shifting responsibility through vague assumptions.
- Strategic Silence: Staying silent in meetings to avoid task assignments while appearing present.
- The Call Strategy: Using calls to avoid written commitments and shift tasks during conversations.
- Testing Market Reactions: Gauging reactions through humor and indirect suggestions.
- Hidden Responsibilities: Indirectly assigning tasks during meetings without clear agreements.

- Using Higher Authority: Leveraging the names of higher-ups to ensure compliance.
- Generic Agreements: Securing vague approvals to cover various scenarios.
- Passing Responsibility: Shifting blame and responsibilities by attributing advice to others.
- New Boss Dynamics: Taking advantage of a new boss to redistribute tasks.
- Saying No: Refusing tasks without offering alternatives, forcing others to find solutions.
- Teamwork Rhetoric: Promoting teamwork while smoothly transitioning responsibilities.
- Minimal Email Communication: Sending concise emails to delegate tasks and avoid detailed explanations.
- Misleading Through Silence: Using non-verbal cues to imply task ownership.
- Assigning Unrelated Tasks: Indirectly delegating tasks by accusing others of being responsible.
- Sales Dynamics: Balancing sales efforts with support tasks to ensure comprehensive coverage.
- Constraints Management: Delegating constraints management to avoid dealing with limitations directly.
- Adaptive Communication: Flipping words to adapt to the situation.
- Navigating Family-Run Businesses: Managing internal politics and unique challenges in family-run businesses.

By understanding and anticipating these tactics, you can navigate your workplace more effectively, avoid falling into common traps, and foster a more positive and productive work environment. This book is not just a guide to surviving difficult colleagues and bosses but a manual for thriving despite them.

**Disclaimer:** The scenarios and characters described in this book, although based on actual events or stories, are fictional and not intended to reference any real individuals. This content is strictly for entertainment purposes. Any resemblance to actual persons, living or dead, is purely coincidental.

# CHAPTER 1: IMPROVING PRODUCTIVITY

**1. Understanding Productivity in Workplace Dynamics**

Productivity is often hailed as the holy grail of workplace success. It's the measure of how efficiently tasks are completed and goals are achieved within a given timeframe. In a collaborative environment, productivity isn't just about individual performance; it involves how well teams coordinate and complement each other's efforts.

However, the drive to maximize productivity can sometimes lead to practices that are less about efficiency and more about shifting burdens. Understanding the nuances of workplace productivity helps us discern between genuine efficiency improvements and tactics that merely redistribute work unfairly.

**2. Strategies for Redistributing Work**

In many workplaces, certain individuals or departments find ways to offload their responsibilities onto others. This can create an illusion of high productivity for some while unfairly increasing the workload for others. Here are some common strategies used to redistribute work:

**Taking from Person/Dept and Pushing to Others**

One of the most prevalent tactics is taking tasks from one person or department and subtly pushing them onto another. This can be done in several ways:

  1. **Delegating Under the Guise of Collaboration:**
     ◦ **The Setup:** A manager or colleague frames the

redistribution of tasks as a collaborative effort. They might say, "We need to work together on this project," but in reality, they are assigning you the bulk of the work.
- **Impact:** This approach can make it difficult to refuse, as it is positioned as a team effort. You might find yourself handling tasks that should have been distributed more evenly.

2. **Feigning Incompetence or Overload:**
   - **The Setup:** A common tactic is to pretend not to understand a task or to claim to be overwhelmed with current responsibilities. This prompts others to take over to avoid delays.
   - **Impact:** This not only increases the workload of the helpful colleague but also sets a precedent for future task dodging.

3. **Highlighting Critical Priorities:**
   - **The Setup:** By emphasizing the urgency or critical nature of certain tasks, a manager can convince others to take on additional responsibilities. They might say, "This is crucial and needs your expertise," while in reality, they are avoiding the task themselves.
   - **Impact:** This creates a sense of obligation and urgency, making it hard for others to refuse.

4. **Selective Delegation:**
   - **The Setup:** Certain tasks are delegated selectively to specific individuals or departments under the pretext of their unique capabilities or lesser workload.
   - **Impact:** This can lead to an imbalance where certain team members are consistently overburdened, affecting their productivity and morale.

## Practical Example: The Overloaded Team

Imagine a scenario in a corporate setting where the marketing department is swamped with multiple campaigns. The head of marketing, seeking to alleviate the pressure on their team, approaches the product development team and says, "We really need your help with the market research for these new campaigns. You guys are great at this." While it appears to be a compliment and a call for collaboration, it essentially pushes additional work onto the product development team, which may already have its hands full.

In this example, the head of marketing effectively redistributes the workload under the guise of seeking expertise, impacting the overall productivity of the product development team.

**Tips for Handling Redistributed Work**

1. **Clarify Roles and Responsibilities:**
   - Before taking on additional tasks, clarify your role and the expectations. Ask specific questions about why the task is being reassigned and whether it aligns with your primary responsibilities.
2. **Set Boundaries:**
   - Learn to say no or negotiate deadlines and workload when additional tasks are pushed onto you. It's essential to set boundaries to ensure that your productivity and job satisfaction are not compromised.
3. **Communicate Transparently:**
   - Open communication with your manager and team about your current workload can help prevent unfair redistribution. Highlight the impact of additional tasks on your productivity and the potential risks involved.
4. **Document Everything:**
   - Keep records of task assignments, deadlines, and responsibilities. Documentation can help in case of disputes and provide clarity on task ownership.
5. **Seek Support:**
   - If you find yourself consistently overburdened due to task redistribution, seek support from HR or higher management. It's important to

address these issues before they escalate and affect your performance and well-being.

Understanding the dynamics of productivity and the strategies used to redistribute work is crucial in maintaining a balanced and fair work environment. By recognizing these tactics, you can better navigate your workplace, protect your workload, and contribute effectively to your team's success.

# CHAPTER 2: THE "I DON'T KNOW" MINDSET

## 1. The Short-Term Memory Approach

The "I Don't Know" mindset is a tactic that revolves around feigning ignorance or short-term memory loss to avoid responsibility or the need to assist others. This approach leverages the convenience of claiming not to remember or know something, even if it is within one's realm of expertise or something frequently encountered. By doing so, individuals can sidestep tasks, questions, and responsibilities, shifting the burden onto others.

This mindset is particularly effective because it capitalizes on the natural human tendency to avoid confrontation and the assumption that people genuinely forget or are unaware. In a fast-paced work environment, colleagues might be more inclined to accept an "I don't know" response and seek assistance elsewhere, rather than pushing back or insisting on an answer.

## 2. Application of the "I Don't Know" Tactic

The "I Don't Know" tactic can be employed in various scenarios within the workplace, especially when others seek help or information. Here's how it typically plays out:

### When Others Ask for Help

1. **Pretending Ignorance:**
    - **Scenario:** A colleague approaches you for assistance on a task you have done multiple times.

- **Tactic:** You respond with, "I don't know," or "I'm not sure how to do that," even though you are well-versed in the task.
- **Impact:** The colleague is forced to find someone else to help or figure it out on their own, effectively removing the burden from you.

2. **Claiming Short-Term Memory Loss:**
   - **Scenario:** During a project meeting, someone asks for details on a process you frequently handle.
   - **Tactic:** You say, "I can't recall the specifics right now," or "I don't remember how we did that last time."
   - **Impact:** The team must spend additional time and resources to revisit or re-explain the process, while you avoid the immediate responsibility.

3. **Deflecting Detailed Requests:**
   - **Scenario:** A new team member asks for a step-by-step guide on a routine task.
   - **Tactic:** You claim, "I don't have that information," or "I'm not familiar with the details."
   - **Impact:** The new team member may seek help from another colleague or spend more time searching for the information themselves, relieving you from the task of mentoring or providing detailed explanations.

**Practical Example: The Elusive Expert**

Consider a scenario where a senior developer, Alex, is frequently approached by junior developers for guidance on coding issues. Instead of assisting them, Alex often responds with, "I'm not sure about that," or "I don't have that information right now." Over time, the junior developers learn to stop approaching Alex for help and either solve their issues independently or seek assistance from more approachable colleagues.

In this example, Alex successfully avoids the responsibility of mentoring and providing support by consistently using the "I don't know" tactic. This not only shifts the workload away from Alex but also discourages others from seeking help in the future.

**Tips for Dealing with the "I Don't Know" Mindset**

1. **Verify Claims:**
    - When you receive an "I don't know" response, especially from someone who should be knowledgeable, politely ask for confirmation or suggest looking up the information together.
2. **Encourage Documentation:**
    - Promote the creation of documentation and knowledge-sharing within the team. This reduces reliance on individuals and makes information more accessible to everyone.
3. **Follow Up:**
    - If you suspect someone is using the "I don't know" tactic to avoid responsibility, follow up with them later. This can either prompt them to provide the needed information or confirm their lack of knowledge.
4. **Provide Training:**
    - Ensure that all team members have adequate training and resources. This can reduce instances where people genuinely don't know how to perform tasks and help identify those who might be using the tactic to avoid work.
5. **Create a Supportive Environment:**
    - Foster a culture where seeking and providing help is encouraged and valued. When everyone feels supported, there is less incentive to use avoidance tactics like "I don't know."

By understanding and recognizing the "I don't know" mindset, you can better navigate workplace dynamics and ensure that responsibilities and tasks are fairly distributed. This awareness helps maintain a productive and cooperative work environment, where everyone is accountable and willing to contribute.

# CHAPTER 3: THE "ALREADY TOLD YOU" TACTIC

**1. Effective Communication with Minimal Effort**

In any workplace, effective communication is crucial for productivity and collaboration. However, some individuals employ a tactic known as the "Already Told You" approach to minimize their efforts while still appearing communicative. This tactic involves providing the bare minimum amount of information, often in a brief and vague manner, and later claiming they have already shared the necessary details when questions arise.

The "Already Told You" tactic can be frustrating for those on the receiving end, as it forces them to decipher incomplete information or repeatedly seek clarification. It creates a veneer of efficiency while subtly shifting the burden of understanding and follow-up onto others.

**2. Strategies for Minimalistic Information Sharing**

There are several strategies that individuals use to implement the "Already Told You" tactic. These strategies focus on providing just enough information to deflect immediate questions, while ensuring that any gaps in understanding are attributed to the recipients.

**Sharing Few Liners or Documents**

1. **The Brief Email:**
    - **Scenario:** A manager needs to convey instructions for a new project.

- **Tactic:** The manager sends an email with a few brief lines of instruction, such as, "Start the new project. Use the template. Follow the guidelines discussed in the last meeting."
- **Impact:** The email lacks specific details, leading team members to either make assumptions or continually seek clarification. When they do, the manager can respond with, "I already told you in the email."

2. **The Comprehensive but Vague Document:**
    - **Scenario:** A colleague is asked to share information about a complex process.
    - **Tactic:** The colleague provides a lengthy document that contains a mix of relevant and irrelevant information, without clear context or guidance.
    - **Impact:** Recipients must sift through the document to find the necessary details. When they ask for specific clarifications, the colleague can say, "I already gave you the document."

3. **The Quick Meeting Recap:**
    - **Scenario:** After a meeting, a team member is responsible for summarizing the key points and action items.
    - **Tactic:** The team member sends out a recap with minimal details, such as, "Discussed project updates. Agreed on next steps. Refer to the meeting notes."
    - **Impact:** The lack of specific details forces others to remember or interpret the meeting's discussions on their own. When they seek further information, the team member can claim, "I already told you in the recap."

### Practical Example: The Master of Minimalism

Imagine a project manager, Jamie, who frequently uses the "Already Told You" tactic. Jamie sends out project briefs that are intentionally sparse, containing just a few bullet points with general instructions. Whenever team members ask for more details, Jamie points them back to the original brief, insisting that everything needed was already provided.

In meetings, Jamie often refers to previous emails or documents, claiming that all necessary information has been shared before. This forces the team to spend extra time trying to piece together incomplete information, while Jamie avoids the effort of providing thorough explanations.

**Tips for Dealing with the "Already Told You" Tactic**

1. **Request Specifics:**
   - When you receive vague or minimalistic communication, ask for specific details upfront. For example, "Can you clarify which template we should use and where I can find the guidelines?"
2. **Document Requests:**
   - Keep a record of all requests for clarification and the responses received. This can help you track what information has actually been provided and challenge the "Already Told You" claim if necessary.
3. **Summarize Understanding:**
   - After receiving minimal information, summarize your understanding in a reply and ask for confirmation. For instance, "To confirm, you want us to start the project using the template found in the shared folder and follow the guidelines from our meeting on June 1st, correct?"
4. **Follow Up:**
   - If the initial communication is insufficient, don't hesitate to follow up with additional questions. Persistence can sometimes prompt more detailed responses.
5. **Encourage Detailed Documentation:**
   - Promote a culture of detailed and thorough documentation within your team. This can help reduce reliance on minimalistic

communication and ensure everyone has access to the information they need.

By understanding and recognizing the "Already Told You" tactic, you can better navigate workplace communication challenges and ensure that important details are not overlooked. This awareness helps maintain clarity and efficiency in your work environment, where everyone has the information they need to succeed.

# CHAPTER 4: FEIGNING IGNORANCE

Feigning ignorance, or pretending not to understand something, can be a powerful tactic used by some individuals to delegate tasks and shift responsibilities. This chapter explores the concept of feigning ignorance and provides practical examples of how it is used in the workplace.

## 1. The Power of "I Don't Understand"

Feigning ignorance involves using phrases like "I don't understand" or "I don't get it" to appear confused or unaware of how to proceed with a task. This tactic can be particularly effective because it often prompts others to step in and take over the task, thereby alleviating the workload of the person pretending to be confused.

The power of this tactic lies in its ability to exploit the helpful nature of colleagues and supervisors. Most people are inclined to assist someone who appears to be struggling or genuinely confused, which makes this approach an easy way to delegate unwanted tasks.

**Key Aspects of Feigning Ignorance:**

1. **Creating Doubt:**
    - By expressing confusion, the individual creates doubt about their ability to complete the task. This often leads others to either take over the task or provide step-by-step instructions.
2. **Encouraging Oversight:**
    - When someone repeatedly claims not to understand, it can lead to others closely monitoring and guiding them through

the task. This reduces the individual's responsibility and effort required.
3. **Shifting Focus:**
    - The tactic shifts the focus from the individual's competence to the immediate need to get the task done. Colleagues and supervisors may prioritize task completion over assessing the individual's understanding.

## 2. Practical Examples of Using Confusion to Delegate Tasks

Here are some practical examples illustrating how feigning ignorance can be used to delegate tasks effectively:

### Example 1: The Confused Report

- **Scenario:** Alex is asked to prepare a complex report for an upcoming meeting.
- **Tactic:** Alex repeatedly tells the supervisor, "I'm not sure I understand how to structure this report. Could you show me how it's done?"
- **Impact:** The supervisor, wanting to ensure the report is done correctly and on time, decides to take over the task or provide detailed guidance, effectively reducing Alex's workload.

### Example 2: The Unclear Instructions

- **Scenario:** Taylor is given a set of instructions to configure a new software system.
- **Tactic:** Taylor responds with, "I'm having trouble understanding these instructions. Can someone show me step-by-step?"
- **Impact:** A colleague steps in to demonstrate the process, or the task is reassigned to someone else more familiar with the software, relieving Taylor of the responsibility.

### Example 3: The Complicated Process

- **Scenario:** Jamie is assigned a task involving a complicated multi-step process.

- **Tactic:** Jamie claims, "This process is really confusing to me. I don't understand how to start."
- **Impact:** The team leader or a colleague takes the time to explain each step in detail or handles the more challenging parts themselves, reducing Jamie's involvement.

**Example 4: The Technical Issue**

- **Scenario:** Morgan is responsible for fixing a technical issue that requires specific expertise.
- **Tactic:** Morgan states, "I don't really understand the technical details of this problem. Can someone else handle it?"
- **Impact:** A technically skilled colleague or IT specialist is called in to resolve the issue, thereby shifting the responsibility away from Morgan.

**Tips for Dealing with Feigning Ignorance**

1. **Clarify Expectations:**
   - When assigning tasks, be clear about expectations and provide detailed instructions. This reduces opportunities for feigned confusion.
2. **Encourage Initiative:**
   - Foster a culture where employees are encouraged to take initiative and seek out information independently before asking for help.
3. **Provide Training:**
   - Ensure that all team members receive adequate training for their tasks. This reduces genuine confusion and highlights when someone might be feigning ignorance.
4. **Follow Up:**
   - When someone claims not to understand, follow up to ensure they are making an effort to learn and improve their understanding.

5. **Document Processes:**
   - Create detailed documentation for processes and procedures. This serves as a reference for those claiming confusion and helps identify when someone might be avoiding responsibility.

By understanding the tactic of feigning ignorance, you can better recognize when it is being used and implement strategies to address it. This ensures that tasks are completed efficiently and that responsibilities are appropriately distributed within your team.

# CHAPTER 5: THE "MY JOB IS DONE" APPROACH

The "My Job is Done" approach is a tactic where individuals quickly complete tasks to a minimal standard, then pass them on to others for review and correction. This chapter explores methods for quick task completion and strategies for transferring responsibility to recipients.

## 1. Quick Task Completion Methods

This approach involves swiftly wrapping up tasks without thorough consideration or quality checks. The goal is to mark the task as "complete" as quickly as possible and move it off one's plate. Here are some common methods used:

**Method 1: Bare Minimum Effort**

- **Description:** Completing only the essential parts of the task, leaving out detailed work or thorough checks.
- **Example:** A report is filled out with only the main points and lacks supporting data or analysis.
- **Impact:** The task appears done at first glance, but it requires significant additional work to meet proper standards.

**Method 2: Generic Templates**

- **Description:** Using pre-existing templates or past work to complete new tasks quickly.
- **Example:** Submitting a proposal by copying a previous

one with minimal modifications.
- **Impact:** While efficient, this method often leads to errors or omissions that need correction.

**Method 3: Assumptive Responses**
- **Description:** Making assumptions to fill in gaps without verifying information.
- **Example:** Completing a form based on assumed data rather than confirming accuracy.
- **Impact:** The work gets completed faster, but inaccuracies require recipients to identify and correct them.

**Method 4: Superficial Reviews**
- **Description:** Performing only a cursory review of the work before declaring it done.
- **Example:** Quickly scanning a document for obvious errors without a detailed read-through.
- **Impact:** Errors or incomplete sections are overlooked, shifting the burden to the recipient.

## 2. Responsibility Transfer: Getting Recipients to Review and Correct Work

Once the initial task is quickly completed, the next step is to transfer the responsibility of quality control and completion to others. Here are strategies for effectively transferring this responsibility:

**Strategy 1: Delegating Review Tasks**
- **Description:** Sending the completed task to a recipient with instructions to review and provide feedback.
- **Example:** "I've drafted the report, can you please review it and let me know if there are any changes needed?"
- **Impact:** The recipient becomes responsible for identifying and correcting errors, effectively doing part of the original task.

## Strategy 2: Prompting for Detailed Feedback

- **Description:** Asking the recipient to point out specific areas that need correction or improvement.
- **Example:** "I've filled out the main sections, could you check the details and let me know if everything aligns?"
- **Impact:** This shifts the responsibility of ensuring accuracy and completeness to the recipient.

## Strategy 3: Invoking Collaboration

- **Description:** Framing the task as a collaborative effort, even if the initial work was done solo.
- **Example:** "I've made a start on this, let's work together to finalize it."
- **Impact:** The recipient feels a sense of shared responsibility and is more likely to contribute to refining the task.

## Strategy 4: Using Authority Figures

- **Description:** Citing instructions or standards from higher-ups to justify the need for a review.
- **Example:** "I've completed the draft as per the initial guidelines, but can you review it to ensure it meets the final standards set by our supervisor?"
- **Impact:** The recipient is compelled to take action, especially if they believe the request aligns with higher authority expectations.

## Strategy 5: Highlighting Potential Issues

- **Description:** Pointing out possible areas of concern that the recipient should pay attention to.
- **Example:** "I've finished the task, but there might be a few things that need double-checking, can you take a look?"
- **Impact:** The recipient is alerted to potential problems and feels responsible for addressing them.

## Tips for Dealing with the "My Job is Done" Approach

1. **Set Clear Expectations:**
   - Clearly outline the standards and requirements for task completion. This reduces the likelihood of tasks being declared complete prematurely.
2. **Implement Checklists:**
   - Use checklists to ensure all aspects of a task are covered before it is considered complete. This helps maintain quality and thoroughness.
3. **Encourage Ownership:**
   - Foster a culture of ownership where individuals are accountable for the entire process, not just the initial completion.
4. **Provide Constructive Feedback:**
   - When reviewing work, provide specific feedback and encourage a learning mindset. This helps improve future task completion.
5. **Document Processes:**
   - Maintain detailed documentation of processes and expectations. This serves as a reference and reduces misunderstandings about task completion.

By understanding the "My Job is Done" approach, you can better recognize when it is being used and implement strategies to ensure tasks are completed to the required standard from the start. This helps maintain productivity and quality within the workplace.

# CHAPTER 6: COUNTERING BY ASKING

The "Countering by Asking" tactic involves responding to questions or requests by making the requestor think for you or provide the answers themselves. This chapter delves into the strategies of deflecting questions by asking them back or using detailed questions to shift the burden of thinking and solving problems to the other person.

## 1. Making the Requestor Think for You

In this strategy, when someone asks you a question or requests your help, instead of providing a direct answer, you prompt them to think about the solution themselves. This can be particularly useful when you don't know the answer or don't want to invest time and effort in figuring it out.

### Method 1: Asking for Suggestions

- **Description:** When approached with a question, respond by asking the requestor for their suggestions or ideas on how to address the issue.
- **Example:** "That's a great question. What do you think would be the best approach to solve this?"
- **Impact:** This shifts the responsibility back to the requestor, making them think through the problem and often providing the answer themselves.

### Method 2: Redirecting to Resources

- **Description:** Instead of answering directly, guide the requestor to resources or references where they can find the information.
- **Example:** "I'm not sure off the top of my head, but have you checked the project documentation or our knowledge base?"
- **Impact:** This encourages self-sufficiency and reduces the need for you to provide immediate answers.

**Method 3: Collaborative Thinking**

- **Description:** Frame the problem as something that requires joint effort, prompting the requestor to contribute ideas.
- **Example:** "Let's think this through together. What steps do you think we should take first?"
- **Impact:** This approach promotes collaboration and distributes the cognitive load.

## 2. Techniques for Deflecting Questions

Deflecting questions effectively involves turning the question back on the requestor or asking detailed questions that guide them to the solution. Here are some techniques to master this tactic:

**Technique 1: Asking Back**

- **Description:** Directly respond to a question with another question that prompts the requestor to think deeper or reconsider their approach.
- **Example:**
    - Requestor: "How should we handle this issue?"
    - You: "What options have you considered so far?"
- **Impact:** This makes the requestor re-evaluate their thoughts and often leads them to the answer independently.

**Technique 2: Detailed Questions**

- **Description:** Ask specific, detailed questions that require the requestor to think critically about the problem and its potential solutions.
- **Example:**
    - Requestor: "Can you help me with this report?"
    - You: "Sure, what specific sections do you need help with, and what data do you already have?"
- **Impact:** By breaking down the problem into smaller parts, the requestor is guided through the process of finding a solution.

## Technique 3: Clarification Questions

- **Description:** Ask for clarification on the request to make the requestor think through the details and potentially solve the problem on their own.
- **Example:**
    - Requestor: "Can you explain how this system works?"
    - You: "Which part of the system are you struggling with specifically?"
- **Impact:** This narrows down the focus, often leading the requestor to identify the solution or at least better articulate their need.

## Technique 4: Future-Oriented Questions

- **Description:** Pose questions that make the requestor consider the long-term implications or outcomes of their actions.
- **Example:**
    - Requestor: "Should we implement this new process?"
    - You: "How do you think this will impact our team's productivity in the long run?"
- **Impact:** This encourages strategic thinking and self-assessment by the requestor.

**Practical Tips for Using the "Countering by Asking" Tactic**
1. **Stay Curious:**
    - Maintain a curious and inquisitive tone when asking back. This keeps the conversation constructive and avoids coming off as evasive.
2. **Encourage Exploration:**
    - Use this tactic to foster a culture of exploration and problem-solving, encouraging team members to seek answers independently.
3. **Balance the Load:**
    - Ensure that you are not overusing this tactic to the point of shirking responsibilities. Use it judiciously to promote self-reliance without neglecting your duties.
4. **Provide Guidance:**
    - When necessary, provide some guidance or hints to steer the requestor in the right direction, ensuring they don't feel completely unsupported.
5. **Follow Up:**
    - After deflecting a question, follow up to see how the requestor managed the task. This shows you are supportive and provides an opportunity for learning and feedback.

By mastering the "Countering by Asking" tactic, you can effectively manage inquiries and requests without overextending yourself. This approach not only helps in distributing the cognitive load but also promotes a proactive and self-sufficient work environment.

# CHAPTER 7: SELECTIVE HEARING

Selective hearing is a tactic used in the workplace to ignore unwanted input or feedback that doesn't align with one's goals or interests. This chapter explores how individuals use selective hearing to manage their workload and interactions and provides insights into recognizing and countering this behavior.

**1. Ignoring Unwanted Input**

Ignoring unwanted input involves selectively filtering out information or feedback that is deemed unimportant or inconvenient. This tactic allows individuals to focus on their priorities while avoiding additional tasks or criticism.

**Scenario 1: The Overloaded Manager**

- **Description**: A manager is already overwhelmed with tasks and decides to ignore additional input from team members that would require extra work or changes in plans.
- **Example**: During a meeting, a team member suggests a new approach to a project that would require significant adjustments. The manager pretends not to hear and continues with the original plan.
- **Impact**: The team member feels ignored and unvalued, and potentially valuable input is lost.

**Scenario 2: The Resistant Colleague**

- **Description**: A colleague who is resistant to change or new ideas may use selective hearing to avoid engaging

with suggestions that disrupt their routine.
- **Example**: When someone proposes a new tool or process to improve efficiency, the resistant colleague dismisses the idea by not acknowledging it.
- **Impact**: Innovation is stifled, and the team may miss out on opportunities for improvement.

**Scenario 3: The Self-Focused Employee**
- **Description**: An employee focused solely on their own tasks and goals may ignore feedback or requests that don't directly benefit them.
- **Example**: A colleague asks for help on a project, but the self-focused employee pretends not to hear and continues with their work.
- **Impact**: Collaboration suffers, and team dynamics are weakened.

## 2. Methods for Pretending You Didn't Hear

There are various methods individuals use to pretend they didn't hear unwanted input, allowing them to sidestep additional responsibilities or feedback.

**Method 1: The Strategic Pause**
- **Description**: Deliberately pausing or not responding immediately to create the impression that the input wasn't heard.
- **Example**: When someone makes a suggestion in a meeting, the person using selective hearing waits a few moments before changing the subject.
- **Impact**: The suggestion is overlooked without direct confrontation.

**Method 2: The Conversation Shift**
- **Description**: Quickly changing the topic of conversation to avoid addressing the input.
- **Example**: A team member brings up a potential issue,

and the person using selective hearing immediately starts talking about an unrelated topic.
- **Impact**: The issue is ignored, and the conversation moves on without resolution.

### Method 3: The Physical Distraction

- **Description**: Using physical actions to signal that the input wasn't heard or isn't important.
- **Example**: Checking emails, looking at a phone, or shuffling papers when someone is speaking.
- **Impact**: The speaker feels dismissed, and their input is disregarded.

### Method 4: The Non-Commital Acknowledgment

- **Description**: Providing a vague or non-committal response that doesn't engage with the input.
- **Example**: Responding with "I'll think about it" or "Let's discuss this later" without any intention of revisiting the topic.
- **Impact**: The input is acknowledged superficially but ultimately ignored.

### Method 5: The Meeting Exit

- **Description**: Leaving the meeting or conversation at a strategic moment to avoid addressing the input.
- **Example**: Claiming to have another urgent commitment right when an inconvenient topic is raised.
- **Impact**: The discussion is cut short, and the input is left unaddressed.

## Recognizing and Countering Selective Hearing

To counter selective hearing in the workplace, it's essential to recognize the signs and adopt strategies to ensure that valuable input is acknowledged and considered.

### Recognizing Selective Hearing:

1. Lack of Response: Notice if the person often fails to respond to suggestions or feedback.
2. Frequent Topic Changes: Observe if the person frequently changes the subject when certain topics are raised.
3. Physical Distractions: Pay attention to body language, such as looking at a phone or appearing disinterested.
4. Vague Acknowledgments: Be aware of non-committal responses that don't engage with the input.

**Countering Selective Hearing:**

1. Direct Follow-Up: Address the input directly and ask for specific feedback or a response. "I noticed we didn't get to discuss your thoughts on this. Can we revisit it now?"
2. Document Discussions: Keep a written record of suggestions and feedback to refer back to and ensure they are acknowledged.
3. Seek Clarification: If you sense you're being ignored, ask for clarification or a decision. "Can we confirm if this is something we can implement?"
4. Involve Others: Bring in other team members to support the input and create a collective voice that is harder to ignore.
5. Set Clear Agendas: In meetings, set clear agendas that include time for discussing feedback and suggestions, making it harder to overlook these topics.

By understanding and recognizing the tactic of selective hearing, you can better navigate workplace dynamics and ensure that valuable input is heard and addressed, fostering a more inclusive and responsive work environment.

# CHAPTER 8: KEEPING THINGS VOCAL

In the realm of workplace dynamics, keeping communication strictly oral is a tactic used by some individuals to avoid accountability and create a flexible narrative. This chapter delves into the strategy of maintaining oral communication and the consequences that arise from a lack of written records.

**1. The Oral Communication Strategy**

Oral communication, while essential for fostering immediate interaction and quick decision-making, can be manipulated by those who wish to avoid accountability. By relying solely on spoken words, individuals can create situations where agreements and decisions become ambiguous and unverifiable.

**Scenario 1: The Ambiguous Agreement**

- **Description:** A manager holds a meeting where several tasks are delegated orally, but no minutes or written records are kept.
- **Example:** During the meeting, the manager vaguely assigns responsibilities, leaving room for interpretation. Later, they can deny or alter the details of what was discussed.
- **Impact:** Team members are left uncertain about their tasks, and the manager can shift blame or change directives without consequence.

**Scenario 2: The Verbal Assurance**

- **Description:** A colleague gives verbal assurances or

promises regarding project support or resources but avoids putting anything in writing.

- **Example:** When asked for confirmation in writing, the colleague insists that everything was already agreed upon verbally.
- **Impact:** The lack of written confirmation leaves the requester without concrete evidence, making it difficult to hold the colleague accountable.

### Scenario 3: The Informal Chat

- **Description:** Important discussions are held in informal settings, such as over coffee or during casual office conversations, with no official documentation.
- **Example:** Decisions made during these chats are later contested or forgotten, as there is no official record.
- **Impact:** Projects suffer from a lack of clarity and direction, leading to potential delays and misunderstandings.

## 2. Consequences of No Records and No Accountability

The deliberate avoidance of written communication can lead to significant issues within a team or organization. The absence of records creates an environment where accountability is undermined, and individuals can evade responsibility.

### Consequence 1: Lack of Clarity

- **Description:** Without written records, team members may have different interpretations of the same discussion or agreement.
- **Example:** Two team members recall a meeting differently, leading to conflicting actions and wasted efforts.
- **Impact:** Confusion and miscommunication can derail projects and reduce overall productivity.

### Consequence 2: Evasion of Responsibility

- **Description:** Individuals can deny their commitments or shift blame onto others when there is no written proof of their promises or decisions.
- **Example:** A manager denies agreeing to a deadline extension that was discussed verbally, putting pressure back on the team.
- **Impact:** Trust within the team erodes, and morale suffers as team members feel unsupported and unfairly treated.

**Consequence 3: Inconsistent Follow-Through**

- **Description:** Without a written trail, it becomes challenging to track progress and ensure that tasks are completed as agreed.
- **Example:** A colleague verbally agrees to complete a task but later claims they misunderstood or forgot the agreement.
- **Impact:** Projects may experience delays and inefficiencies due to inconsistent follow-through.

**Consequence 4: Manipulation of Narratives**

- **Description:** Individuals can manipulate verbal agreements to suit their interests, changing the story to their advantage when convenient.
- **Example:** A colleague insists that a task was never assigned to them, despite verbal discussions to the contrary.
- **Impact:** The integrity of project management is compromised, and the team's ability to deliver on objectives is weakened.

**Strategies to Counter the Oral Communication Tactic**

To counter the tactic of keeping things vocal and ensure accountability, it's important to implement strategies that promote transparency and clarity.

## Strategy 1: Insist on Written Records

- **Action:** After important discussions, follow up with an email summarizing the key points and agreements.
- **Example:** "Following our meeting today, here is a summary of the tasks we discussed and the deadlines agreed upon."
- **Benefit:** Creates a written record that can be referenced later to ensure accountability.

## Strategy 2: Document Meeting Minutes

- **Action:** Designate a person to take detailed notes during meetings and distribute the minutes to all attendees.
- **Example:** "Attached are the minutes from our last meeting. Please review and confirm the tasks assigned."
- **Benefit:** Provides a clear and official record of decisions and assignments.

## Strategy 3: Request Written Confirmations

- **Action:** Ask for written confirmation of any verbal agreements or decisions.
- **Example:** "Can you please confirm in writing the new deadline we discussed?"
- **Benefit:** Ensures there is a concrete record of commitments that can be enforced.

## Strategy 4: Use Collaboration Tools

- **Action:** Utilize project management and collaboration tools that automatically log communication and task assignments.
- **Example:** Tools like Asana, Trello, or Slack that provide a transparent log of all actions and discussions.
- **Benefit:** Enhances visibility and accountability across the team.

## Strategy 5: Formalize Informal Discussions

- **Action:** After informal discussions, send a follow-up email summarizing the key points and any agreed-upon actions.
- **Example:** "To recap our coffee chat, we agreed that you will handle the client presentation. Please let me know if I missed anything."
- **Benefit:** Transforms informal discussions into formal records that can be referenced.

By recognizing and addressing the tactic of keeping things vocal, teams can foster a culture of accountability and transparency, ensuring that all members are on the same page and responsible for their commitments.

# CHAPTER 9: SAYING YOU UNDERSTAND

In the workplace, appearing competent and knowledgeable is crucial for maintaining a positive professional image. However, some individuals exploit this need by feigning understanding during meetings and then seeking clarification later. This chapter explores the tactic of saying "I understand" to appear competent and the strategies for following up to gain the necessary information.

### 1. Appearing Competent in Meetings

Appearing competent in meetings is often associated with nodding in agreement, affirming understanding, and refraining from asking questions that might reveal a lack of knowledge. This behavior is employed by individuals who want to avoid looking uninformed or unprepared in front of their peers and superiors.

**Scenario 1: The Confident Nod**

- **Description:** An employee nods along during a meeting, giving the impression that they fully grasp the concepts being discussed.
- **Example:** During a technical briefing, the employee nods at each point made by the presenter, signaling understanding and agreement.
- **Impact:** Colleagues and superiors perceive the employee as knowledgeable and engaged, even if the employee is unsure about the details.

**Scenario 2: Affirmative Responses**

- **Description:** An individual frequently uses phrases like

"I understand" or "Got it" during discussions to indicate comprehension.

- **Example:** In a strategy session, the employee repeatedly says "I understand" to convey competence and avoid probing questions.
- **Impact:** The employee appears confident and capable, preventing any immediate scrutiny of their actual understanding.

**Scenario 3: Avoiding Questions**

- **Description:** To avoid revealing their lack of knowledge, an employee refrains from asking clarifying questions in the meeting.
- **Example:** During a project update, the employee avoids asking questions about unclear aspects of the plan to maintain their appearance of competence.
- **Impact:** The meeting proceeds smoothly without interruptions, but the employee leaves with unresolved questions.

## 2. Follow-Up Strategies for Seeking Clarification

After the meeting, individuals who feigned understanding need to gather the necessary information to perform their tasks effectively. This section outlines strategies for seeking clarification without undermining the initial impression of competence.

**Strategy 1: One-on-One Follow-Up**

- **Action:** Approach a colleague or team member privately to ask for clarification on specific points.
- **Example:** "Hey, I wanted to make sure I understood everything from the meeting. Can you explain the new process we discussed?"
- **Benefit:** Allows for detailed explanations without the pressure of a group setting.

**Strategy 2: Reviewing Meeting Materials**

- **Action:** Carefully review any materials, minutes, or recordings from the meeting to fill in knowledge gaps.
- **Example:** Re-reading the slide deck or listening to the recorded meeting to better understand the discussed topics.
- **Benefit:** Provides a second chance to grasp the information without needing to ask questions publicly.

### Strategy 3: Asking Targeted Questions

- **Action:** Send a follow-up email with specific, targeted questions to clarify unclear points.
- **Example:** "Can you clarify the timeline for the new project phase mentioned in the meeting? I want to ensure I have the correct dates."
- **Benefit:** Demonstrates attention to detail and a proactive approach to gaining understanding.

### Strategy 4: Using Collaborative Tools

- **Action:** Utilize project management or collaboration tools to ask questions and seek clarification from the team.
- **Example:** Posting questions on a team Slack channel or within a project management platform like Asana.
- **Benefit:** Encourages a collaborative environment where team members can share knowledge and insights.

### Strategy 5: Scheduling a Briefing

- **Action:** Request a brief follow-up meeting or one-on-one session with a knowledgeable colleague or manager.
- **Example:** "Can we schedule a quick 15-minute call to go over the new reporting requirements? I want to make sure I'm clear on the expectations."
- **Benefit:** Provides an opportunity for in-depth clarification and direct communication.

## Practical Examples

### Example 1: The New System Implementation

- **Scenario:** During a meeting about a new software system, an employee nods and says they understand the implementation process. Later, they realize they need more details.
- **Follow-Up:** They schedule a one-on-one with the IT specialist to walk through the steps in detail, ensuring they can competently execute their tasks.

### Example 2: The Marketing Strategy Update

- **Scenario:** In a marketing strategy meeting, an employee affirms their understanding of the new campaign approach. After the meeting, they have questions about the specific tactics.
- **Follow-Up:** They review the meeting materials and then send a targeted email to the marketing manager asking for clarification on the campaign timeline and target metrics.

### Example 3: The Project Milestone Discussion

- **Scenario:** During a project milestone discussion, an employee avoids asking questions about the new deadlines to avoid looking uninformed.
- **Follow-Up:** They use the project management tool to review the updated timelines and then post specific questions in the project chat for additional clarification.

By employing the tactic of saying "I understand" during meetings and following up with strategic questions afterward, individuals can maintain their appearance of competence while ensuring they have the necessary information to perform their tasks effectively. This approach balances the need to look knowledgeable with the practical requirement of gaining a thorough understanding of the work at hand.

# CHAPTER 10: THE POWER OF ASSUMPTIONS

In the workplace, the ability to navigate complex dynamics often involves more than just completing tasks; it includes managing perceptions and responsibilities. One subtle yet powerful tactic used by some individuals is leveraging assumptions to shift responsibility. This chapter delves into the strategy of using assumptions effectively and provides examples of how it can be applied in areas such as risk assessment and calculations.

## 1. Using "Assume" Effectively to Shift Responsibility

The word "assume" can be a strategic tool in the hands of those looking to shift responsibility and avoid accountability. By making assumptions explicit, individuals can imply that others have already considered important factors, thereby shifting the burden of oversight and responsibility onto them.

**Scenario 1: Project Deadlines**

- **Description:** An employee communicates a project deadline by saying, "I assumed you had factored in the holiday schedule when setting the deadlines."
- **Impact:** This statement implies that any delays or oversights related to the holiday schedule are the responsibility of the person who set the deadlines, not the one making the assumption.

**Scenario 2: Budget Management**

- **Description:** During a budget meeting, someone might

say, "I assumed the finance team had already allocated funds for this initiative."

- **Impact:** This shifts the responsibility for budget shortfalls or misallocations to the finance team, distancing the speaker from any financial oversight issues.

**Scenario 3: Task Delegation**

- **Description:** When delegating tasks, a manager might say, "I assumed you had the necessary resources to complete this task."
- **Impact:** If the task fails due to lack of resources, the responsibility falls on the employee for not flagging the issue, rather than on the manager for not ensuring adequate support.

**Scenario 4: Client Expectations**

- **Description:** In client interactions, an account manager might state, "I assumed the client was aware of the limitations of this service."
- **Impact:** If the client is dissatisfied, the blame is shifted to the client for not understanding the service limitations, rather than on the account manager for not clearly communicating them.

## 2. Examples in Risk and Calculations

Assumptions are particularly potent in areas involving risk and calculations, where the stakes are high, and the details are critical. Here are some examples of how assumptions can be used to shift responsibility in these contexts.

**Example 1: Risk Assessment**

- **Scenario:** During a risk assessment meeting, a team member says, "I assumed you had included all potential risk factors in your analysis."
- **Impact:** This places the responsibility for any overlooked risks on the person who conducted the

analysis, rather than the speaker.

**Example 2: Financial Calculations**

- **Scenario:** When reviewing financial projections, someone might say, "I assumed you had accounted for all market fluctuations in these calculations."
- **Impact:** Any errors or omissions in the financial projections are attributed to the person who prepared them, not the one making the assumption.

**Example 3: Quality Control**

- **Scenario:** In a quality control review, an employee states, "I assumed the production team had already conducted the necessary tests."
- **Impact:** Any quality issues discovered later are seen as the production team's oversight, not the individual who made the assumption.

**Example 4: Project Planning**

- **Scenario:** During a project planning session, a project manager might declare, "I assumed the team leaders had already synchronized their timelines."
- **Impact:** Any scheduling conflicts or misalignments are blamed on the team leaders, not the project manager.

**Practical Examples**

**Example 1: New Software Implementation**

- **Scenario:** In a meeting about implementing new software, an IT manager says, "I assumed you had checked the compatibility with our existing systems."
- **Impact:** If compatibility issues arise, the responsibility is shifted to the person who was supposed to check compatibility.

**Example 2: Marketing Campaign Analysis**

- **Scenario:** During a marketing campaign review, a team member mentions, "I assumed the data you provided included all recent trends."

- **Impact:** If the campaign analysis is flawed, the blame is placed on the person who provided the data, not the analyst.

**Example 3: Customer Support Issue**

- **Scenario:** When addressing a customer support problem, a supervisor states, "I assumed you had followed up with the client as we discussed."
- **Impact:** Any unresolved issues with the client are seen as the responsibility of the person who was supposed to follow up.

**Example 4: Product Development**

- **Scenario:** In a product development meeting, a designer says, "I assumed the product specifications were final."
- **Impact:** If the specifications change, any resulting design issues are attributed to the assumption that they were final, shifting responsibility away from the designer.

By strategically using assumptions, individuals can navigate workplace dynamics more effectively, shifting responsibility and avoiding direct accountability for potential oversights or mistakes. This tactic, while potentially manipulative, is a common method used to manage perceptions and responsibilities in a professional setting.

# CHAPTER 11: STRATEGIC SILENCE

In the intricate dance of workplace dynamics, sometimes saying less can be more. Strategic silence is a tactic employed by individuals who prefer to stay under the radar, avoiding unnecessary attention or responsibility while still making their presence known when it matters. This chapter explores how staying quiet in meetings and speaking only when necessary can be used as a powerful tool to navigate the workplace.

## 1. Staying Under the Radar in Meetings

Meetings are a common aspect of professional life, where ideas are exchanged, decisions are made, and responsibilities are assigned. For some, these gatherings are an opportunity to shine, but for others, they are a minefield of potential pitfalls. Those who employ strategic silence understand the value of minimizing their involvement to avoid drawing attention or being burdened with additional tasks.

**Scenario 1: Passive Participation**

- **Description:** Attending meetings with a focus on listening rather than contributing. By nodding and occasionally making supportive noises, one can appear engaged without actively participating.
- **Impact:** This approach allows individuals to remain informed while avoiding the spotlight. They can gather information and insights without being held accountable for contributions or decisions made during the meeting.

**Scenario 2: Non-Verbal Communication**

- **Description:** Utilizing body language such as nodding, smiling, and maintaining eye contact to show engagement without speaking up.
- **Impact:** Non-verbal cues can convey participation and agreement without the need for verbal input. This helps maintain a presence without the risks associated with voicing opinions or suggestions.

### Scenario 3: Selective Note-Taking

- **Description:** Taking detailed notes during meetings without participating in discussions. This can be presented as a reason for silence.
- **Impact:** By focusing on note-taking, individuals can justify their silence as a necessary part of their role. This keeps them out of direct conversations and responsibilities that may arise from them.

### Scenario 4: Strategic Questions

- **Description:** Asking a few well-placed, strategic questions towards the end of the meeting to show attentiveness.
- **Impact:** This tactic allows individuals to maintain an appearance of involvement and understanding while still minimizing their overall participation. It also places them in a position to clarify points without committing to additional tasks.

### 2. Speaking Only When Necessary

While staying silent can be beneficial, there are moments when speaking up is unavoidable. The key is to do so strategically, ensuring that every word counts and contributes to a positive perception without leading to additional responsibilities.

### Scenario 1: Marking Attendance

- **Description:** Speaking up only when required to mark attendance, such as during roll calls or when directly addressed.

- **Impact:** This minimal participation ensures that one's presence is noted without contributing to the workload or being dragged into discussions.

**Scenario 2: Providing Minimal Input**

- **Description:** Offering brief, non-committal input when directly asked for an opinion. Responses such as "I agree," "Sounds good," or "Let's consider it" are effective.
- **Impact:** These types of responses show engagement without deeply involving oneself in the conversation or decision-making process.

**Scenario 3: Clarifying Questions**

- **Description:** Asking clarifying questions that highlight understanding and attention but do not lead to additional work. For example, "Can you please elaborate on that point?" or "How does this affect our current project?"
- **Impact:** Clarifying questions demonstrate engagement and comprehension while avoiding the trap of taking on new responsibilities or tasks.

**Scenario 4: Strategic Agreement**

- **Description:** Agreeing with the majority opinion or aligning with the boss's viewpoint to avoid conflict and maintain a positive perception.
- **Impact:** This tactic helps in staying aligned with team dynamics without contributing new ideas or objections that could lead to more work or conflict.

**Practical Examples**

**Example 1: Project Meetings**

- **Scenario:** During a project meeting, an employee remains silent for most of the discussion, only speaking up to confirm their attendance and agree with the project leader's summary.

- **Impact:** The employee appears engaged and supportive without being assigned additional tasks or responsibilities.

**Example 2: Departmental Reviews**

- **Scenario:** In a departmental review, an individual listens attentively, taking notes and asking a single clarifying question towards the end.
- **Impact:** This approach shows they are paying attention and contributing thoughtfully, without being overly involved in discussions that could lead to more work.

**Example 3: Team Brainstorming Sessions**

- **Scenario:** During a brainstorming session, an employee contributes one or two ideas early on, then remains silent for the rest of the meeting.
- **Impact:** This ensures their participation is noted, but they avoid the potential of being assigned to develop or lead the implementation of ideas.

**Example 4: Client Meetings**

- **Scenario:** In a client meeting, an account manager speaks only to provide necessary updates and agrees with the client's suggestions, deferring detailed discussions to follow-up emails.
- **Impact:** The manager maintains a professional and cooperative stance while keeping the door open to handle specifics later, potentially in a more controlled environment.

By mastering the art of strategic silence, individuals can effectively navigate the complexities of workplace dynamics. This tactic allows them to stay informed and appear engaged without taking on additional responsibilities or drawing unnecessary attention. When used wisely, strategic silence can be a powerful tool for managing one's role and workload in any professional setting.

# CHAPTER 12: THE CALL STRATEGY

In the modern workplace, communication is key to getting things done. However, some individuals use communication tactics to push work, blame, or responsibility onto others. One such tactic is the call strategy, which involves avoiding written communication and using quick calls to delegate work. This chapter delves into how this strategy is employed and the impact it can have on workplace dynamics.

**1. Avoiding Written Communication**

Written communication, such as emails and documents, creates a paper trail that holds individuals accountable. To sidestep this, some people prefer to handle discussions and task delegations through verbal communication. This approach allows them to avoid direct responsibility and leaves little to no record of the conversation.

**Scenario 1: Immediate Call Requests**

- **Description:** When someone sends an email asking for assistance or clarification, the individual quickly responds by suggesting a phone call instead of addressing the query in writing.
- **Impact:** This move prevents any written record of the discussion, making it easier to deny commitments or twist the conversation later if needed.

**Scenario 2: Vague Meeting Minutes**

- **Description:** After a verbal discussion, the person either does not document the meeting or writes vague minutes that lack specific details.

- **Impact:** This creates ambiguity about what was agreed upon, allowing the individual to reinterpret or deny agreements if questioned later.

**Scenario 3: Deflecting Responsibility**

- **Description:** During verbal conversations, the individual avoids making clear commitments, using phrases like "let's discuss this further" or "we can look into it."
- **Impact:** This tactic avoids direct responsibility and leaves room for the individual to deflect blame or claim misunderstanding later on.

## 2. Execution of Quick Calls to Delegate Work

Quick calls are often used to delegate tasks or shift responsibilities onto others without leaving a clear trail. This method can be particularly effective in high-pressure environments where decisions are made rapidly, and detailed follow-up is often lacking.

**Scenario 1: Immediate Task Delegation**

- **Description:** When assigned a task via email, the individual immediately calls a colleague to verbally delegate the task, often without informing the original sender.
- **Impact:** The verbal delegation leaves no written record, making it difficult for the original sender to track the progress or verify who is responsible.

**Scenario 2: Miscommunication Claims**

- **Description:** After a verbal delegation, the individual can later claim there was a miscommunication or that the task was not understood correctly.
- **Impact:** This creates confusion and allows the individual to avoid blame for incomplete or poorly executed tasks.

## Scenario 3: Pushing Responsibility During Calls

- **Description:** The individual uses phone calls to push complex or undesirable tasks onto others by suggesting that they are better suited for the job or have more capacity.
- **Impact:** This shifts the workload onto others without clear documentation, making it hard for the recipient to push back or claim overburdening.

## Scenario 4: Follow-Up Ambiguity

- **Description:** After delegating tasks via call, the individual may follow up with vague or non-specific questions, avoiding direct accountability for the task's progress.
- **Impact:** This maintains the ambiguity around who is responsible for the task, allowing the individual to shift blame if necessary.

## Practical Examples

### Example 1: Project Assignments

- **Scenario:** A project manager receives a new assignment via email but immediately calls a team member to discuss the task, subtly suggesting they handle it.
- **Impact:** The verbal suggestion is not documented, leaving the team member responsible without a clear assignment in writing.

### Example 2: Meeting Follow-Ups

- **Scenario:** After a meeting, instead of sending detailed follow-up emails, the manager calls team members individually to discuss their tasks, avoiding written records.
- **Impact:** This approach prevents the creation of a clear action plan and makes it easier to deny or alter responsibilities later.

### Example 3: Blame Shifting

- **Scenario:** When a task goes wrong, the individual claims in a call that they had delegated the task verbally and there was a misunderstanding.
- **Impact:** This tactic allows the individual to shift blame to the team member without clear evidence of the original assignment.

### Example 4: High-Pressure Situations

- **Scenario:** In a high-pressure situation, the individual uses quick calls to make rapid decisions and delegate tasks, ensuring there is no time to document the process.
- **Impact:** This results in a lack of accountability and a trail of undocumented decisions, making it difficult to hold the individual responsible for outcomes.

By understanding and recognizing the call strategy, individuals can better navigate these tactics and ensure that communication and responsibility are clear and documented. This helps maintain accountability and prevents the misuse of verbal communication to shift blame or workload unfairly.

# CHAPTER 13: TESTING MARKET REACTIONS

In the workplace, some individuals employ subtle and indirect tactics to push work, blame, or responsibility onto others. One such tactic is "testing market reactions," which involves using humor or casual remarks to gauge reactions and test boundaries. This chapter explores how this strategy is used and provides practical examples of its implementation.

## 1. Using Humor to Gauge Reactions

Humor can be a powerful tool in the workplace. It can diffuse tension, build rapport, and make communication more approachable. However, it can also be used strategically to gauge reactions and subtly push tasks or responsibilities onto others.

### Scenario 1: Joking About Responsibilities

- **Description:** An individual makes a joke about someone else taking on a task or responsibility, testing their willingness or readiness to accept it.
- **Example:** "Hey, maybe you can handle the client presentation next week since you're so good at talking!"
- **Impact:** This lighthearted approach allows the individual to gauge the other person's reaction without making a direct request, leaving room to escalate the suggestion if the response is positive.

### Scenario 2: Casual Remarks About Workload

- **Description:** The person casually comments on their own workload in a humorous way, suggesting that

others might help out.
- **Example:** "I feel like I'm juggling a thousand balls here—anybody want to catch a few?"
- **Impact:** This creates an opening for colleagues to offer help, effectively shifting some of the workload without making an explicit request.

**Scenario 3: Testing Ideas Through Humor**
- **Description:** An individual uses humor to propose new ideas or changes, gauging the team's openness to these suggestions.
- **Example:** "Wouldn't it be hilarious if we all switched roles for a day? Imagine how much fun that would be!"
- **Impact:** This tests the team's reaction to potential changes, providing insight into their flexibility and openness without making a formal proposal.

## 2. Implementation of Testing Boundaries

Testing boundaries involves making subtle, often humorous suggestions or comments to see how far responsibilities can be pushed onto others without resistance. This tactic helps individuals understand their colleagues' limits and find opportunities to delegate tasks or shift blame.

**Scenario 1: Suggesting Additional Tasks**
- **Description:** The individual humorously suggests that a colleague take on an additional task or responsibility during a casual conversation.
- **Example:** "Hey, since you're already handling the reports, why not add the budget analysis to your plate? Just kidding... unless you're up for it!"
- **Impact:** This tests the colleague's willingness to take on more work, making it easier to push the task onto them if they respond positively.

**Scenario 2: Testing Reaction to Criticism**

- **Description:** The person humorously criticizes a process or decision to see how others react, potentially shifting blame or responsibility.
- **Example:** "Whoever came up with this filing system must have been having a bad day. Should we blame Bob for this mess? Just kidding, Bob!"
- **Impact:** This gauges how others respond to criticism and can subtly shift the focus or blame away from the individual making the comment.

**Scenario 3: Proposing Changes Lightly**

- **Description:** The individual proposes changes or new ideas in a lighthearted manner to test their acceptance without facing immediate pushback.
- **Example:** "Imagine if we changed our meeting times to 7 AM—who's in? Just kidding, but seriously, how do we feel about earlier meetings?"
- **Impact:** This approach allows the individual to gather feedback on potential changes without committing to them, providing valuable insights into the team's preferences.

**Scenario 4: Delegating Through Humor**

- **Description:** The person uses humor to delegate tasks, making it seem like a fun or easy thing to do, thereby reducing resistance.
- **Example:** "You know, organizing the team outing is such a fun task! How about you take the lead on that? You'll be great at it!"
- **Impact:** This creates a positive perception of the task and reduces the likelihood of pushback, making it easier to delegate responsibilities.

**Practical Examples**

**Example 1: Team Projects**

- **Scenario:** During a team meeting, an individual jokes about someone else taking the lead on a new project.
- **Example:** "Oh, come on, you're the project guru around here! This one's all yours—I'm just here for the snacks!"
- **Impact:** The humor softens the suggestion, making it easier for the other person to accept the responsibility without feeling pressured.

**Example 2: Feedback Sessions**

- **Scenario:** An individual uses humor to test the team's reaction to feedback or new ideas during a feedback session.
- **Example:** "Imagine if we scrapped the whole project and started fresh—who's with me? Just kidding, but seriously, any thoughts on how we can improve?"
- **Impact:** This approach encourages open discussion and provides insights into the team's readiness for changes without creating tension.

**Example 3: Workload Distribution**

- **Scenario:** The person humorously suggests that a colleague take on additional tasks during a casual conversation.
- **Example:** "You're like a productivity machine! How about taking over the inventory reports too? Just kidding... or am I?"
- **Impact:** This tests the colleague's willingness to take on more work, making it easier to delegate if the response is positive.

By understanding and recognizing the tactic of testing market reactions, individuals can better navigate these subtle strategies and maintain clear boundaries. This helps prevent the unfair delegation of tasks and ensures that responsibilities are distributed more equitably.

# CHAPTER 14: HIDDEN RESPONSIBILITIES

In many workplaces, there are individuals who excel at pushing tasks, blame, or responsibility onto others without drawing attention to their actions. One of their tactics is to assign hidden responsibilities, often through subtle methods that go unnoticed until it's too late. This chapter explores how these hidden responsibilities are assigned and provides practical examples of agenda manipulation to achieve this goal.

### 1. Assigning Tasks Under the Radar

Assigning tasks under the radar involves subtly adding responsibilities to someone's plate without a formal announcement or clear communication. This tactic allows individuals to delegate work without facing immediate resistance or scrutiny.

**Scenario 1: Casual Mentions**

- **Description:** During a casual conversation or a meeting, someone casually mentions that a task needs to be done, subtly implying that the listener should take it on.
- **Example:** "By the way, we need someone to handle the client feedback for this quarter. Can you look into that?"
- **Impact:** The task is assigned without a formal request, making it harder for the recipient to refuse.

**Scenario 2: Implicit Expectations**

- **Description:** Responsibilities are assigned through implied expectations rather than explicit instructions.

- **Example:** "I'm sure you'll do a great job on the budget review, just like you did last time!"
- **Impact:** The recipient feels obligated to take on the task due to implied expectations based on past performance.

### Scenario 3: Follow-Up Emails

- **Description:** After a meeting or conversation, follow-up emails are sent summarizing tasks and subtly adding new responsibilities that were not explicitly discussed.
- **Example:** "Great meeting today! Just to recap, please handle the project report, and also, let's start preparing for the upcoming audit."
- **Impact:** The new task is hidden within a summary, making it seem like a natural extension of the discussed duties.

### Scenario 4: Overloading Through Delegation

- **Description:** Tasks are distributed among team members in a way that overloads specific individuals while appearing fair.
- **Example:** "Since you're already managing the marketing campaign, can you also take charge of the social media updates? It makes sense to keep it all together."
- **Impact:** The recipient ends up with a heavier workload, often without realizing the extent of the additional responsibilities.

## 2. Methods for Agenda Manipulation

Agenda manipulation involves subtly altering the agenda of meetings or discussions to include additional tasks or responsibilities for others. This method allows the assigner to delegate tasks without facing immediate resistance or scrutiny.

### Scenario 1: Adding Items Mid-Meeting

- **Description:** During a meeting, new tasks are introduced without prior notice, catching participants off guard.

- **Example:** "Before we wrap up, there's one more thing. Can we discuss the upcoming event planning?"
- **Impact:** Participants are less likely to object to new tasks introduced at the last minute, feeling pressured to agree.

**Scenario 2: Hidden Agendas in Meeting Invites**

- **Description:** Meeting invites contain vague descriptions, with the actual agenda including additional responsibilities not mentioned beforehand.
- **Example:** "Meeting to discuss project updates" becomes a session to assign new tasks.
- **Impact:** Attendees are unprepared for the additional responsibilities, making it harder to refuse.

**Scenario 3: Post-Meeting Summaries**

- **Description:** After a meeting, a summary is sent out that includes additional tasks not explicitly agreed upon during the discussion.
- **Example:** "As discussed, here are the action items: ... Also, please prepare the financial analysis for our next meeting."
- **Impact:** The new task is presented as a continuation of the meeting, creating an obligation to comply.

**Scenario 4: Combining Tasks**

- **Description:** Multiple smaller tasks are combined into one larger task, making it appear as a single responsibility.
- **Example:** "Let's bundle the event coordination with the marketing strategy—you can handle both since they're related."
- **Impact:** The recipient is overloaded with a larger task that includes hidden responsibilities.

## Practical Examples

### Example 1: Team Meetings

- **Scenario:** During a team meeting, a manager subtly introduces a new responsibility without making it an official agenda item.
- **Example:** "By the way, can someone volunteer to take notes? It'll help with our documentation process."
- **Impact:** The task of note-taking is assigned casually, making it hard for anyone to refuse without seeming uncooperative.

**Example 2: Project Kick-Offs**

- **Scenario:** At the start of a new project, the project lead casually mentions additional responsibilities for team members.
- **Example:** "While we're at it, can you also handle the client communications? It's just a small addition."
- **Impact:** The new responsibility is added under the radar, with team members feeling obliged to accept.

**Example 3: Email Follow-Ups**

- **Scenario:** After a discussion, an email summary includes tasks that were not clearly assigned during the meeting.
- **Example:** "Thanks for the productive meeting. As we discussed, please start working on the new market analysis and coordinate with the sales team."
- **Impact:** The new task is hidden within the summary, making it harder for recipients to push back.

By recognizing these tactics of assigning hidden responsibilities and agenda manipulation, individuals can better navigate their workplace dynamics. This awareness helps prevent unfair delegation and ensures that tasks and responsibilities are clearly communicated and fairly distributed.

# CHAPTER 15: USING HIGHER AUTHORITY

In the intricate web of workplace dynamics, leveraging higher authority to assign tasks, blame, or responsibility is a common tactic. This strategy involves using the names or implied approval of senior managers or executives to push work onto others. By invoking higher authority, the assigner can avoid direct confrontation and increase the likelihood of compliance. This chapter delves into how this tactic is employed and provides strategies for recognizing and managing such situations.

**1. Leveraging Authority to Assign Tasks**

When someone invokes the name or authority of a higher-up, it adds weight to the request, making it harder to refuse. This method is particularly effective because it creates a perception of importance and urgency.

**Scenario 1: Direct Name-Dropping**

- **Description:** Tasks are assigned by directly mentioning that a senior manager or executive has requested the action.
- **Example:** "John asked me to have you prepare the quarterly report."
- **Impact:** The recipient feels pressured to comply due to the perceived importance of the request.

**Scenario 2: Implicit Authority**

- **Description:** The task assigner implies that the directive comes from higher up without explicitly stating it.

- **Example:** "This needs to be done quickly; the higher-ups are keeping an eye on this project."
- **Impact:** The recipient is led to believe that senior management is involved, increasing the perceived urgency.

### Scenario 3: Email CCs

- **Description:** Including senior managers in the CC line of emails to add pressure on the recipient to comply with the request.
- **Example:** "Can you handle this by Friday? CC: John Doe, Senior Manager."
- **Impact:** The recipient feels more obligated to complete the task due to the visibility of the request.

### Scenario 4: Quoting Past Conversations

- **Description:** Referring to previous discussions with senior management to validate the task assignment.
- **Example:** "During our last meeting, Sarah mentioned we should prioritize this. Can you take care of it?"
- **Impact:** The recipient feels that there is a directive from higher authority, even if it was a general mention.

## 2. Strategies for Indirect Authority

Indirect authority involves more subtle tactics, where the pressure to comply with task assignments comes from implied approval or indirect references to senior management.

### Scenario 1: Reference to Company Goals

- **Description:** Assigning tasks by linking them to broad company goals or initiatives that have the backing of senior management.
- **Example:** "This is critical for our Q4 goals. Can you take the lead on this?"
- **Impact:** The recipient feels the weight of company-wide priorities, making it harder to refuse.

## Scenario 2: Using Policy as a Shield

- **Description:** Assigning tasks by citing company policies or procedures that are presumed to have the support of higher management.
- **Example:** "According to our new policy, we need to have this done by next week. Can you handle it?"
- **Impact:** The recipient feels compelled to follow through due to the legitimacy of policy.

## Scenario 3: Highlighting Consequences

- **Description:** Emphasizing potential negative outcomes or repercussions that would attract the attention of senior management.
- **Example:** "If we don't get this done, it might cause issues for our department, and we know how much scrutiny we're under."
- **Impact:** The recipient is motivated to act to avoid negative consequences and scrutiny.

## Scenario 4: Shared Responsibility

- **Description:** Creating a sense of shared responsibility by including oneself in the task, while subtly shifting the bulk of the work to the recipient.
- **Example:** "We need to ensure this report is flawless for the board meeting. Can you draft it, and I'll review it?"
- **Impact:** The recipient feels a collaborative effort but ends up doing most of the work.

## Practical Examples

## Example 1: Team Project

- **Scenario:** During a project kickoff meeting, the project lead uses the name of a senior executive to assign tasks.
- **Example:** "Jane from the executive team emphasized the importance of this project. Can you lead the data analysis?"

- **Impact:** The team member feels compelled to accept due to the implied importance from a senior executive.

### Example 2: Urgent Email

- **Scenario:** An urgent task is assigned via email with senior management copied in.
- **Example:** "Please prioritize this task and complete it by EOD. CC: Senior Manager."
- **Impact:** The visibility of the email to senior management adds pressure on the recipient to comply.

### Example 3: Policy Changes

- **Scenario:** During a department meeting, a manager assigns tasks by referring to recent policy changes.
- **Example:** "With the new compliance guidelines, we need this report updated immediately. Can you handle it?"
- **Impact:** The recipient feels obligated due to the legitimacy of policy changes backed by higher authority.

### Example 4: Preparing for Reviews

- **Scenario:** In preparation for a quarterly review, tasks are delegated by highlighting potential scrutiny from senior management.
- **Example:** "We need to be thorough in our preparations for the review. Can you ensure all documents are updated and accurate?"
- **Impact:** The recipient feels the pressure of potential scrutiny and is motivated to comply.

By understanding these tactics of leveraging higher authority and employing indirect authority, individuals can better navigate workplace dynamics. Recognizing these strategies allows for more informed decision-making and helps in managing responsibilities more effectively.

# CHAPTER 16: GENERIC AGREEMENTS

In the workplace, securing blanket approvals through vague or generic agreements can be an effective tactic to push work, blame, or responsibility onto others. This chapter explores the strategies used to obtain such approvals and how to recognize and handle them.

## 1. Securing Blanket Approvals

Securing blanket approvals involves getting someone to agree to a broad or nonspecific request, which can then be used to cover a wide range of tasks or responsibilities. This tactic relies on the recipient's lack of attention to detail and the ambiguity of the request.

**Scenario 1: Vague Requests**

- **Description:** Making broad, nonspecific requests that seem harmless but can be interpreted in multiple ways later.
- **Example:** "Can you handle this project?" without specifying the scope or details.
- **Impact:** The recipient agrees without fully understanding what they are committing to, allowing the assigner to shift various responsibilities later.

**Scenario 2: General Approvals**

- **Description:** Seeking approval for a general concept or idea, which can later be used to justify specific actions or assignments.

- **Example:** "Do you agree that we need to improve our department's efficiency?" which can later be interpreted as approval for implementing numerous initiatives.
- **Impact:** The recipient's general agreement can be used as a blanket approval for various tasks, reducing the need for further consultation.

### Scenario 3: Implicit Agreements

- **Description:** Phrasing requests in a way that implies agreement is already expected or has been given.
- **Example:** "We're all on the same page about this, right?" without giving a clear opportunity for dissent.
- **Impact:** The recipient feels pressured to agree, and this perceived consensus can be leveraged for future assignments.

### Scenario 4: Broad Endorsements

- **Description:** Obtaining endorsements for broad goals or missions that can be later interpreted to cover specific tasks.
- **Example:** "We need everyone's support to make this quarter successful," which can be used to justify assigning extra work.
- **Impact:** The recipient's endorsement of the general goal is used to validate specific actions without further discussion.

## 2. Techniques for One-Liner Questions

One-liner questions are concise, often oversimplified queries designed to elicit a quick yes or no answer. These questions can be strategically used to obtain generic agreements without delving into details, making it easier to shift responsibilities later.

### Scenario 1: Simple Yes/No Questions

- **Description:** Asking straightforward yes/no questions that don't provide enough context for an informed decision.

- **Example:** "Can you handle this?" without providing specifics.
- **Impact:** The recipient's affirmative response is used to justify assigning various tasks later.

**Scenario 2: Repetition for Confirmation**

- **Description:** Repeating the same simple question to push for a yes or no answer without giving additional information.
- **Example:** "Is it okay if we proceed?" even if the recipient asks for more details, the question remains the same.
- **Impact:** The recipient feels pressured to give a quick response, which is then used as a blanket approval.

**Scenario 3: Leading Questions**

- **Description:** Phrasing questions in a way that leads the recipient towards a particular answer.
- **Example:** "You agree that this is important, right?" implying that disagreement would be unreasonable.
- **Impact:** The recipient feels compelled to agree, providing the assigner with a broad approval to act on.

**Scenario 4: Urgent Requests**

- **Description:** Framing the question as urgent to elicit a quick agreement without proper consideration.
- **Example:** "Can you approve this right now?" creating a sense of urgency.
- **Impact:** The recipient gives a hasty approval, which can be used to justify further actions.

## Practical Examples

### Example 1: Project Endorsement

- **Scenario:** A manager asks for a quick endorsement of a project without detailing the full scope.
- **Example:** "Do you support this new project?" leading to

an agreement that is later used to assign extensive tasks.
- **Impact:** The recipient's broad approval is used to justify additional work assignments.

### Example 2: Efficiency Improvements
- **Scenario:** During a meeting, a team leader seeks agreement on the need for efficiency improvements.
- **Example:** "Do you agree we need to be more efficient?" which is later used to implement various changes without further consultation.
- **Impact:** The general agreement on efficiency is used to support specific actions and assignments.

### Example 3: Consensus Building
- **Scenario:** A team member seeks a quick consensus on a minor issue to leverage it for broader tasks.
- **Example:** "Can we all agree this needs to be done?" followed by assigning related tasks to those who agreed.
- **Impact:** The perceived consensus is used to distribute responsibilities without detailed discussion.

### Example 4: Last-Minute Approvals
- **Scenario:** A supervisor asks for a last-minute approval to proceed with a task.
- **Example:** "Is it okay if we move forward with this now?" leading to a hasty agreement that is used to justify multiple actions.
- **Impact:** The rushed approval is used to validate a range of tasks, minimizing the need for further approvals.

By understanding these tactics of securing generic agreements and using one-liner questions, individuals can better navigate workplace dynamics and recognize when they are being subtly manipulated. This awareness allows for more informed decision-making and better management of responsibilities.

# CHAPTER 17: PASSING RESPONSIBILITY

One of the most pervasive tactics in the workplace is the art of passing responsibility. This can take the form of shifting blame when things go wrong or attributing advice and decisions to others to avoid accountability. Understanding these tactics can help you navigate the complexities of workplace dynamics and protect yourself from being unfairly burdened with extra work or blame.

### 1. Shifting Blame and Responsibility

Shifting blame and responsibility involves deflecting accountability for tasks, mistakes, or outcomes onto someone else. This tactic can be subtle or overt, but it always aims to protect the individual from negative consequences.

**Scenario 1: The Blame Game**

- **Description:** When a project fails or a mistake is made, the individual points fingers at others rather than taking responsibility.
- **Example:** "The project was delayed because the marketing team didn't provide the materials on time."
- **Impact:** The individual avoids blame, and the marketing team is left to defend themselves and rectify the issue.

**Scenario 2: The Missing Link**

- **Description:** Assigning blame to someone who is not present to defend themselves.
- **Example:** "I would have completed the report, but John

was supposed to provide the data, and he's out of town."
- **Impact:** The absent person is blamed, and the individual deflects responsibility.

### Scenario 3: Delegating Failure
- **Description:** Assigning a difficult or likely-to-fail task to someone else.
- **Example:** "I think you should handle this client issue. You have a better rapport with them."
- **Impact:** If the task fails, the responsibility lies with the person to whom it was delegated.

### Scenario 4: The Passive-Aggressive Blame
- **Description:** Subtly suggesting that someone else is at fault through indirect comments.
- **Example:** "It's unfortunate that we missed the deadline. It would have helped if everyone had been as committed as some of us."
- **Impact:** This creates division and shifts blame without direct confrontation.

### Scenario 5: Blame by Proxy
- **Description:** Using another's actions or decisions as a scapegoat for one's own failures.
- **Example:** "I followed Jane's advice on this, and it didn't work out as planned."
- **Impact:** Jane is blamed for the failure, protecting the individual who made the decision to follow her advice.

## 2. Execution of Attributing Advice

Attributing advice involves deflecting responsibility for decisions by claiming they were based on someone else's recommendations. This can be an effective way to shield oneself from blame if the outcome is negative.

### Scenario 1: The Expert's Advice

- **Description:** Claiming that a decision was based on an expert's advice to deflect responsibility.
- **Example:** "I made this choice because the consultant suggested it."
- **Impact:** If the decision fails, the blame is shifted to the consultant rather than the decision-maker.

**Scenario 2: Team Consensus**

- **Description:** Stating that a decision was made based on team consensus to avoid individual blame.
- **Example:** "We all agreed in the meeting that this was the best course of action."
- **Impact:** Responsibility is diffused among the team, making it harder to pinpoint individual accountability.

**Scenario 3: The Higher-Up's Directive**

- **Description:** Attributing a decision to instructions from higher management.
- **Example:** "I'm implementing this because our director insisted on it."
- **Impact:** If the outcome is negative, the blame is shifted to higher management rather than the executor.

**Scenario 4: The Predecessor's Plan**

- **Description:** Blaming previous plans or decisions made by someone no longer in the role.
- **Example:** "This was already set in motion by my predecessor, so I had to follow through."
- **Impact:** The predecessor, who is no longer around to defend themselves, takes the blame.

**Scenario 5: The Collective Input**

- **Description:** Asserting that the decision was made based on collective input from multiple sources.
- **Example:** "This approach was recommended by several

of our advisors."
- **Impact:** Responsibility is diluted among the advisors, shielding the individual from direct blame.

## Practical Examples

### Example 1: Failed Project Blame

- **Scenario:** A project fails due to poor planning.
- **Execution:** The project manager claims, "The team decided on this timeline together," shifting the blame to the entire team.
- **Impact:** The manager avoids direct blame, and the team collectively bears the responsibility.

### Example 2: Advice Attribution

- **Scenario:** A marketing strategy does not yield the expected results.
- **Execution:** The marketing head states, "We followed the agency's recommendations," attributing the failure to external advice.
- **Impact:** The marketing head deflects blame onto the agency.

### Example 3: Directive from Above

- **Scenario:** A policy change leads to employee dissatisfaction.
- **Execution:** The HR manager says, "This policy was implemented based on the CEO's directive."
- **Impact:** Blame is shifted to the CEO, protecting the HR manager.

### Example 4: Collective Decision

- **Scenario:** A product launch is delayed.
- **Execution:** The product manager asserts, "We all agreed that delaying the launch was necessary."
- **Impact:** Responsibility is shared among the team,

reducing individual accountability.

**Example 5: Previous Plan Blame**

- **Scenario:** An ongoing project encounters issues.
- **Execution:** The current manager claims, "This plan was already in place before I took over."
- **Impact:** The predecessor is blamed for the problems, shielding the current manager.

By understanding these tactics of passing responsibility and attributing advice, individuals can better protect themselves from unfair blame and ensure that accountability is appropriately assigned. Recognizing these behaviors in others can also help in managing workplace dynamics more effectively.

# CHAPTER 18: NEW BOSS DYNAMICS

When a new boss arrives, it's a period of adjustment and opportunity. Some colleagues might use this transition phase to push work, blame, or responsibility onto others. Understanding these tactics and knowing how to navigate them can help you maintain your position and ensure you don't end up with an unfair share of the workload.

**1. Strategies for Dealing with a New Boss**

New bosses come with their own set of challenges and dynamics. Colleagues may use this time to either impress the new boss or avoid new tasks by redistributing their current responsibilities.

**Strategy 1: Creating a Positive Impression**

- **Tactic:** Colleagues may go out of their way to appear highly competent and proactive.
- **Example:** Offering to take on high-visibility projects or presenting completed tasks that highlight their skills.
- **Impact:** They aim to secure a favorable position with the new boss, possibly at the expense of others who might be left with less desirable tasks.

**Strategy 2: Highlighting Other Departments**

- **Tactic:** Suggesting that certain responsibilities or tasks are better handled by other departments.
- **Example:** "The finance team has more experience with budget analysis, so they should handle this."
- **Impact:** The colleague successfully shifts tasks away

from their own team, reducing their workload while increasing that of another department.

### Strategy 3: Deflecting New Responsibilities

- **Tactic:** Claiming lack of expertise or bandwidth to take on new tasks.
- **Example:** "I'd love to help with the new project, but my current workload is too heavy."
- **Impact:** The colleague avoids new responsibilities, making it likely that someone else will be assigned the task.

### Strategy 4: Leveraging Existing Relationships

- **Tactic:** Using established relationships with other departments to suggest collaborative work.
- **Example:** "We have a good rapport with the IT team; they can manage this integration."
- **Impact:** Tasks are redirected to those with existing relationships, reducing the workload for the colleague's own team.

### Strategy 5: Offering Superficial Help

- **Tactic:** Agreeing to help with a task but only providing minimal assistance.
- **Example:** "I can help with the report, but I'll just review the final draft."
- **Impact:** The colleague appears helpful but avoids the bulk of the work, which is left to others.

## 2. Implementation of Redistributing Tasks

Redistributing tasks during the transition phase with a new boss can be subtle but effective. Here are some common methods used to shift work to others:

### Method 1: Suggesting Expertise-Based Allocation

- **Description:** Recommending that tasks be assigned based on expertise, often exaggerating the other department's capabilities.

- **Example:** "The HR team is excellent at onboarding, so they should handle the new hires."
- **Impact:** This method shifts the workload to those deemed more 'capable,' reducing the burden on the colleague's own team.

## Method 2: Highlighting Workload Imbalance

- **Description:** Pointing out an imbalance in workloads to justify redistributing tasks.
- **Example:** "Our team is currently managing three major projects, whereas the marketing team is only handling one."
- **Impact:** This can prompt the new boss to reallocate tasks to even out the workload, often benefiting the colleague's team.

## Method 3: Proposing Collaborative Efforts

- **Description:** Suggesting collaboration between departments, which often leads to shifting most of the work elsewhere.
- **Example:** "This project requires input from both sales and product development. Let's have the product team take the lead."
- **Impact:** The colleague's team ends up with a reduced role, while the majority of the work is done by another team.

## Method 4: Redefining Job Roles

- **Description:** Redefining roles to include or exclude certain tasks, subtly shifting responsibilities.
- **Example:** "The operations team should handle all logistics-related tasks, as they are more aligned with their role."
- **Impact:** Responsibilities are shifted based on new role

definitions, often lightening the load for the colleague's own team.

**Method 5: Playing the New Boss Card**

- **Description:** Using the new boss's unfamiliarity with the team's capabilities to their advantage.
- **Example:** "Since you're new, I thought it would be best to handle this task in a way that leverages our strengths."
- **Impact:** The new boss may agree, resulting in a redistribution of tasks that favors the colleague's team.

**Practical Examples**

**Example 1: Expertise-Based Allocation**

- **Scenario:** A new boss is assigning roles for an upcoming project.
- **Execution:** A colleague says, "The design team has the most experience with user interface, so they should handle this part."
- **Impact:** The design team gets additional tasks, reducing the load on the colleague's team.

**Example 2: Highlighting Workload Imbalance**

- **Scenario:** The new boss is unaware of current team workloads.
- **Execution:** A colleague points out, "Our team is already stretched thin, but the support team seems less busy."
- **Impact:** The new boss reallocates tasks to the support team, easing the colleague's workload.

**Example 3: Proposing Collaborative Efforts**

- **Scenario:** A collaborative project is being planned.
- **Execution:** A colleague suggests, "Let's have the development team take the lead since they have more resources."
- **Impact:** The development team ends up with the

primary responsibility, reducing the workload for the colleague's team.

**Example 4: Redefining Job Roles**

- **Scenario:** Roles and responsibilities are being reassigned.
- **Execution:** A colleague says, "Given our skill set, it makes sense for the technical team to handle all system integrations."
- **Impact:** The technical team gets additional responsibilities, while the colleague's team is relieved of some tasks.

**Example 5: Playing the New Boss Card**

- **Scenario:** A new boss is making decisions on task allocation.
- **Execution:** A colleague advises, "Based on our past performance, it's best if the analytics team handles all data-related tasks."
- **Impact:** The new boss agrees, leading to a redistribution of tasks that favors the colleague's team.

By recognizing these strategies and methods, you can better navigate the dynamics when a new boss arrives. Stay vigilant and ensure you don't end up with an unfair share of the workload or responsibility.

# CHAPTER 19: SAYING NO

In any workplace, being able to say "no" effectively is a crucial skill. However, some colleagues use this tactic strategically to avoid work, push responsibilities onto others, or simply manage their own workload better. Understanding how to refuse tasks effectively and create alternatives for others can help you navigate these dynamics without falling into their traps.

## 1. Refusing Tasks Effectively

Refusing tasks without appearing uncooperative or negative is an art. Some colleagues have mastered this skill, ensuring they stay on good terms while avoiding additional responsibilities.

**Tactic 1: The Strategic Decline**

- **Description:** Politely declining tasks while offering a plausible reason.
- **Example:** "I'd love to help, but I'm currently tied up with another high-priority project."
- **Impact:** This creates a legitimate excuse, making it hard for others to insist on assigning the task.

**Tactic 2: Overloading Excuse**

- **Description:** Highlighting current workload to justify refusal.
- **Example:** "I'm currently managing several deadlines, so taking this on might affect the quality of my other work."
- **Impact:** This positions the refusal as a concern

for overall quality and efficiency, making it more acceptable.

### Tactic 3: Skill Set Mismatch

- **Description:** Citing lack of expertise or experience as a reason to decline.
- **Example:** "This task seems to require specific skills that I'm not proficient in. It might be better suited for someone else."
- **Impact:** This shifts the focus to finding the right person for the task rather than pushing back against the task itself.

### Tactic 4: Delegating Upwards

- **Description:** Suggesting that the task might need higher-level approval or involvement.
- **Example:** "I think this decision should involve our manager to ensure it aligns with our strategic goals."
- **Impact:** This deflects the task upwards, often leading to reallocation or reconsideration.

### Tactic 5: Conditional Acceptance

- **Description:** Agreeing to take on the task only under certain conditions.
- **Example:** "I can take this on, but I'll need an extension on my current deadlines."
- **Impact:** This positions the acceptance as conditional, often leading to the task being reassigned to avoid complications.

## 2. Creating Alternatives for Others

By suggesting alternatives when refusing tasks, colleagues can maintain their cooperative image while effectively shifting the workload elsewhere.

### Technique 1: Suggesting Other Resources

- **Description:** Pointing out other individuals or teams

better suited for the task.

- **Example:** "I think Jane in the marketing team has handled similar projects before. She might be a great fit for this."
- **Impact:** This helps reassign the task without outright refusal, making the suggestion seem helpful rather than dismissive.

**Technique 2: Proposing Collaborative Efforts**

- **Description:** Suggesting the task be handled by a group rather than an individual.
- **Example:** "This project seems extensive. How about we form a small team to tackle it together?"
- **Impact:** This dilutes the workload across multiple people, reducing individual burden.

**Technique 3: Recommending Automation or Tools**

- **Description:** Suggesting tools or software that can handle the task more efficiently.
- **Example:** "This could be streamlined using the new project management software. It might save us a lot of time."
- **Impact:** This shifts the focus to finding efficient solutions, often leading to task reassignment or adoption of new tools.

**Technique 4: Offering Guidance Instead**

- **Description:** Offering to provide guidance or advice rather than doing the task directly.
- **Example:** "I can't take this on right now, but I'm happy to walk you through the process if you need help."
- **Impact:** This provides support without taking on the full responsibility, often leading to the task being completed by the original requester.

### Technique 5: Redirecting to Documentation

- **Description:** Pointing out existing documentation or resources that can help with the task.
- **Example:** "There's a detailed guide on this in our shared drive. That should have all the information you need."
- **Impact:** This shifts the responsibility back to the requester while appearing helpful.

### Practical Examples

### Example 1: The Strategic Decline

- **Scenario:** A colleague is asked to take on an additional report.
- **Execution:** "I'm currently finalizing the quarterly budget. Can we revisit this after it's submitted?"
- **Impact:** The task is deferred, often leading to it being reassigned or forgotten.

### Example 2: Overloading Excuse

- **Scenario:** A manager asks for help with an urgent presentation.
- **Execution:** "I'm swamped with client meetings this week. How about I assist with the next one?"
- **Impact:** The task is redirected, buying time and potentially shifting it to someone else.

### Example 3: Skill Set Mismatch

- **Scenario:** A technical task is assigned to someone without the relevant skills.
- **Execution:** "This seems like it needs a developer's input. Perhaps Tom from IT can help?"
- **Impact:** The task is reassigned to someone more suitable.

### Example 4: Delegating Upwards

- **Scenario:** A significant project decision needs to be

made.
- **Execution:** "We should get the director's input on this to ensure it aligns with our goals."
- **Impact:** The responsibility is shifted upwards, often leading to a different allocation of the task.

**Example 5: Conditional Acceptance**
- **Scenario:** A colleague is asked to lead a new project.
- **Execution:** "I can take this on if we can extend the deadline for my current project."
- **Impact:** This may lead to task reassignment to avoid disrupting existing deadlines.

By mastering the art of saying no and creating viable alternatives, colleagues can effectively manage their workload and avoid unnecessary responsibilities. Understanding these tactics will help you recognize when they are being used and ensure you don't end up unfairly burdened with extra tasks.

# CHAPTER 20: TEAMWORK RHETORIC

In the workplace, the concept of teamwork is often invoked to foster collaboration and ensure smooth operations. However, some colleagues and bosses may use the rhetoric of teamwork as a strategy to push work, blame, or responsibility onto others. Recognizing and navigating these tactics is essential to protect yourself from being overburdened or unfairly blamed.

## 1. Using Teamwork as a Tool

Teamwork is a powerful and positive concept that emphasizes collaboration and shared goals. However, it can also be manipulated by those looking to offload work or blame onto others.

**Tactic 1: The "We're All in This Together" Approach**

- **Description:** Encouraging a sense of shared responsibility to distribute individual tasks.
- **Example:** "We all need to pitch in to get this done; it's a team effort."
- **Impact:** This creates a sense of collective responsibility, making it difficult for individuals to refuse additional work.

**Tactic 2: Implicit Delegation through Group Tasks**

- **Description:** Assigning tasks to a group without clear individual responsibilities.
- **Example:** "Our team needs to prepare the presentation for Monday."

- **Impact:** This often leads to proactive team members taking on the bulk of the work while others contribute minimally.

**Tactic 3: The Vague Assignment**

- **Description:** Giving broad or unclear assignments under the guise of teamwork.
- **Example:** "Let's all contribute to the project documentation."
- **Impact:** Ambiguity allows the assigner to offload responsibility without direct accountability.

**Tactic 4: Emotional Appeals to Team Spirit**

- **Description:** Using emotional appeals to the concept of team spirit to encourage extra work.
- **Example:** "It's really important for the team's success that we all give 110%."
- **Impact:** This leverages guilt and loyalty to prompt individuals to take on more work.

## 2. Methods for Transitioning Responsibility

Transitioning responsibility in a team setting can be subtle and strategic. Understanding these methods will help you recognize when you are being unfairly burdened and how to manage such situations.

**Method 1: The "On to You" Technique**

- **Description:** Smoothly shifting tasks to another team member at the end of a discussion.
- **Example:** "This is a great start. John, can you take it from here and finalize the details?"
- **Impact:** This often leaves the new assignee feeling obligated to complete the task.

**Method 2: The Praise and Pass**

- **Description:** Complimenting someone's ability before assigning them additional work.

- **Example:** "You're really good at handling these reports. Can you take care of this one as well?"
- **Impact:** The praise makes it harder for the person to refuse the added responsibility.

### Method 3: The Collective Assignment with Hidden Lead

- **Description:** Assigning a task to a group but subtly indicating who should take the lead.
- **Example:** "The team needs to develop the new protocol. Sarah, can you coordinate the initial steps?"
- **Impact:** This pushes the bulk of the responsibility onto the designated coordinator.

### Method 4: The Strategic Absence

- **Description:** Absence from critical stages of a project, forcing others to pick up the slack.
- **Example:** "I'll be out of the office next week. Can someone ensure the project stays on track?"
- **Impact:** This tactic leaves others to manage and complete the tasks during the absence.

### Method 5: The Deferred Follow-Up

- **Description:** Agreeing to help but delaying involvement until the task is nearly complete.
- **Example:** "I can review the final draft once you're done with the initial version."
- **Impact:** This minimizes personal workload while still appearing helpful.

## Practical Examples

### Example 1: The "We're All in This Together" Approach

- **Scenario:** A manager encourages the team to stay late to finish a project.
- **Execution:** "Let's all stay an extra hour today to ensure we meet the deadline. We're in this together!"

- **Impact:** The team feels collective pressure to comply, even if some members have already completed their tasks.

### Example 2: Implicit Delegation through Group Tasks
- **Scenario:** A project requires extensive research.
- **Execution:** "Our team needs to gather all the data for the quarterly review."
- **Impact:** Without specific assignments, the responsibility often falls on the more proactive team members.

### Example 3: The Vague Assignment
- **Scenario:** A broad task is assigned without clear guidance.
- **Execution:** "We need to update the training manual."
- **Impact:** Lack of specifics leads to uneven distribution of effort, with some members doing more than others.

### Example 4: Emotional Appeals to Team Spirit
- **Scenario:** A critical deadline is approaching.
- **Execution:** "We need everyone to put in extra effort to ensure we don't let the team down."
- **Impact:** This leverages emotional appeal to encourage additional, often uncompensated, work.

### Example 5: The "On to You" Technique
- **Scenario:** During a meeting, a task is assigned.
- **Execution:** "I've outlined the main points. Emily, can you handle the rest and finalize it?"
- **Impact:** Emily feels compelled to complete the task as it's been transitioned to her in front of others.

## Conclusion

Understanding how teamwork rhetoric can be used to transition responsibility is key to navigating workplace dynamics effectively.

By recognizing these tactics, you can protect yourself from being unfairly burdened and ensure that responsibilities are appropriately shared within your team. This awareness will help you maintain a balanced workload and foster a healthier work environment.

# CHAPTER 21: MINIMAL EMAIL COMMUNICATION

In the modern workplace, email communication is a vital tool for conveying information and delegating tasks. However, some colleagues and bosses use minimal email communication as a tactic to push work, blame, or responsibility onto others. Understanding these tactics can help you navigate and respond effectively.

## 1. Sending Concise Emails to Delegate Tasks

Minimal email communication involves sending brief, often vague emails that leave much of the task's details and responsibilities open to interpretation. This tactic can be used to offload tasks quickly without providing necessary guidance or clarity.

**Tactic 1: The One-Liner Email**

- **Description:** Sending a very short email with a basic directive.
- **Example:** "Please handle this report."
- **Impact:** The recipient must decipher the task's details and scope, potentially leading to confusion and additional follow-up.

**Tactic 2: The Forwarded Email with Minimal Context**

- **Description:** Forwarding an email with little to no explanation.

- **Example:** Forwarding an email chain with just "FYI" or "Please take care of this."
- **Impact:** The recipient has to read through the entire email chain to understand the context and required actions.

**Tactic 3: The Vague Task Assignment**

- **Description:** Assigning tasks with ambiguous instructions.
- **Example:** "Look into this matter."
- **Impact:** The recipient must guess what specific actions are needed, which can lead to incomplete or incorrect task execution.

**Tactic 4: The Delegation Without Details**

- **Description:** Delegating a task without providing necessary background information or resources.
- **Example:** "Prepare the presentation for the meeting."
- **Impact:** Without details on the meeting's agenda, audience, or required content, the recipient may struggle to complete the task effectively.

## 2. Follow-Up Strategies for Confirming Responsibilities

After sending minimal emails, these colleagues or bosses often employ follow-up strategies to confirm responsibilities and ensure the task is pushed onto the recipient. Recognizing these strategies will help you manage expectations and clarify roles.

**Strategy 1: The Confirmation Email**

- **Description:** Following up with an email to confirm the recipient has understood and accepted the task.
- **Example:** "Just checking if you received my email about the report?"
- **Impact:** This puts pressure on the recipient to acknowledge and take ownership of the task.

**Strategy 2: The Reminder Email**

- **Description:** Sending periodic reminders about the task.
- **Example:** "Just a reminder about the presentation due tomorrow."
- **Impact:** These reminders reinforce the expectation that the recipient is responsible for completing the task.

**Strategy 3: The Escalation Email**

- **Description:** Escalating the task to higher management if there are delays or issues.
- **Example:** "I've noticed the report is still pending. I'll escalate this if it's not done by EOD."
- **Impact:** This tactic uses the threat of escalation to ensure compliance and quick action from the recipient.

**Strategy 4: The Public Follow-Up**

- **Description:** Following up in a group email or meeting to apply social pressure.
- **Example:** "Can we get an update on the report you were handling?"
- **Impact:** This public follow-up creates a sense of urgency and accountability, often pushing the recipient to complete the task promptly.

**Practical Examples**

**Example 1: The One-Liner Email**

- **Scenario:** Delegating a task with minimal effort.
- **Execution:** "Please handle this report."
- **Impact:** The recipient must determine the report's requirements and deadline, often leading to additional clarifications.

**Example 2: The Forwarded Email with Minimal Context**

- **Scenario:** Forwarding an important email without explanation.
- **Execution:** Forwarding an email with "FYI."

- **Impact:** The recipient needs to read through the entire email chain to understand what actions are needed.

## Example 3: The Vague Task Assignment

- **Scenario:** Assigning a task without clear instructions.
- **Execution:** "Look into this matter."
- **Impact:** The recipient must figure out what specific actions to take, leading to potential misunderstandings.

## Example 4: The Delegation Without Details

- **Scenario:** Delegating a complex task without providing necessary background information.
- **Execution:** "Prepare the presentation for the meeting."
- **Impact:** The recipient struggles to complete the task effectively without knowing the meeting's agenda, audience, or required content.

## Example 5: The Confirmation Email

- **Scenario:** Ensuring task acceptance.
- **Execution:** "Just checking if you received my email about the report?"
- **Impact:** The recipient feels pressured to acknowledge and accept the task.

## Example 6: The Reminder Email

- **Scenario:** Reinforcing task responsibility.
- **Execution:** "Just a reminder about the presentation due tomorrow."
- **Impact:** The recipient is reminded of the task's urgency and their responsibility.

## Example 7: The Escalation Email

- **Scenario:** Using escalation to ensure compliance.
- **Execution:** "I've noticed the report is still pending. I'll escalate this if it's not done by EOD."

- **Impact:** The recipient is pushed to complete the task promptly due to the threat of escalation.

### Example 8: The Public Follow-Up

- **Scenario:** Applying social pressure in a group setting.
- **Execution:** "Can we get an update on the report you were handling?"
- **Impact:** The recipient feels a heightened sense of urgency and accountability.

### Conclusion

Minimal email communication can be an effective tactic for those looking to offload work or responsibility quickly. By recognizing these tactics and understanding the follow-up strategies, you can navigate these situations more effectively. Ensure you seek clarity and document responsibilities to protect yourself from being unfairly burdened or blamed. This awareness will help you maintain a balanced workload and foster better communication in the workplace.

# CHAPTER 22: MISLEADING THROUGH SILENCE

In the workplace, silence can be a powerful tool for those looking to push work, blame, or responsibility onto others. By strategically remaining silent or using non-verbal cues, colleagues and bosses can subtly imply task ownership and redirect responsibilities without explicitly stating them. Understanding these tactics will help you recognize when silence is being used against you and how to counter it.

**1. Using Non-Verbal Cues to Imply Task Ownership**

Non-verbal communication can often speak louder than words. In meetings or group discussions, individuals may use silence combined with body language to imply that someone else should take ownership of a task.

**Tactic 1: The Silent Nod**

- **Description:** Nodding in agreement without verbally committing to a task.
- **Example:** In a meeting, someone nods when a task is mentioned, giving the impression they are in agreement but not explicitly taking responsibility.
- **Impact:** Others may assume the task has been accepted by the nodding individual, even though no verbal commitment was made.

**Tactic 2: Avoiding Eye Contact**

- **Description:** Deliberately avoiding eye contact when a task is being assigned.
- **Example:** Looking away or down when a new project is being discussed.
- **Impact:** This can lead others to believe that the person is not involved or uninterested, subtly redirecting the task to someone else who appears more engaged.

**Tactic 3: Passive Agreement**

- **Description:** Remaining silent and giving passive signals of agreement, such as slight nods or non-committal gestures.
- **Example:** Slightly nodding when tasks are distributed but not saying anything.
- **Impact:** This creates ambiguity about who is responsible, often leading others to pick up the task to ensure it gets done.

**Tactic 4: The Blank Stare**

- **Description:** Using a blank or neutral facial expression to avoid showing any reaction.
- **Example:** Maintaining a neutral expression when tasks are being assigned, providing no clues to acceptance or refusal.
- **Impact:** This leaves the responsibility in limbo, often resulting in someone else stepping up to clarify and take on the task.

**2. Techniques for Redirecting Tasks**

Once a task is implied to be someone else's responsibility through silence or non-verbal cues, further tactics can be employed to ensure the task is redirected away from oneself.

**Strategy 1: The Follow-Up Deflection**

- **Description:** When asked about progress on a task, redirecting the question to another team member.

- **Example:** "I think John was looking into that. John, do you have an update?"
- **Impact:** This shifts the focus and responsibility onto someone else, even if the initial task assignment was unclear.

## Strategy 2: The Silent Observer

- **Description:** Remaining silent during discussions about task details and only speaking up to ask questions that imply someone else's responsibility.
- **Example:** "Can you clarify what Sarah's role will be in this project?"
- **Impact:** By framing questions around another person's involvement, the speaker subtly pushes responsibility onto them.

## Strategy 3: The Meeting Ghost

- **Description:** Attending meetings without participating actively, thereby avoiding direct task assignments.
- **Example:** Sitting quietly and only speaking when directly addressed.
- **Impact:** This non-participation can lead to the assumption that the quiet individual is not responsible for any of the tasks discussed.

## Strategy 4: The Late Arriver

- **Description:** Arriving late to meetings where tasks are being assigned, missing the discussion about responsibilities.
- **Example:** Walking in just after roles have been distributed and remaining silent.
- **Impact:** This tactic ensures the person is not directly assigned tasks, as the distribution often happens early in the meeting.

## Practical Examples

### Example 1: The Silent Nod

- **Scenario:** Task assignment in a team meeting.
- **Execution:** Nodding slightly when a task is mentioned without verbally accepting it.
- **Impact:** Team members may assume the task has been accepted, but the nodder hasn't actually committed.

### Example 2: Avoiding Eye Contact

- **Scenario:** Discussion about project roles.
- **Execution:** Looking down or away when a task is brought up.
- **Impact:** Others may interpret this as a lack of interest, redirecting the task to someone else.

### Example 3: Passive Agreement

- **Scenario:** Distributing responsibilities for a new project.
- **Execution:** Slight nods and non-committal gestures without speaking.
- **Impact:** Ambiguity leads others to assume responsibility to avoid project delays.

### Example 4: The Blank Stare

- **Scenario:** Assigning tasks during a team briefing.
- **Execution:** Maintaining a neutral expression when tasks are discussed.
- **Impact:** Creates uncertainty, often resulting in proactive team members taking on the task.

### Example 5: The Follow-Up Deflection

- **Scenario:** Progress check on an assigned task.
- **Execution:** Redirecting the question to another team member.
- **Impact:** Shifts responsibility and focus onto someone else.

### Example 6: The Silent Observer

- **Scenario:** Discussing task details in a meeting.
- **Execution:** Asking questions that imply someone else's responsibility.
- **Impact:** Subtly pushes the task onto another team member.

### Example 7: The Meeting Ghost

- **Scenario:** Participating in a project planning meeting.
- **Execution:** Remaining silent and only speaking when directly addressed.
- **Impact:** Avoids direct task assignments, leaving responsibilities to others.

### Example 8: The Late Arriver

- **Scenario:** Joining a meeting after task distribution.
- **Execution:** Arriving late and staying silent.
- **Impact:** Ensures no direct task assignments, as roles were distributed earlier.

### Conclusion

Misleading through silence is a subtle yet powerful tactic used to push work, blame, or responsibility onto others. By recognizing non-verbal cues and follow-up strategies, you can navigate these situations more effectively. Ensure clear communication and explicitly assign tasks to avoid ambiguity and unfair burden. This awareness will help you maintain fairness and accountability in the workplace, fostering a more transparent and efficient working environment.

# CHAPTER 23: AGREEMENT BY CALL

In the workplace, securing agreements over calls can be an effective strategy for pushing work, blame, or responsibility onto others. Unlike written communication, calls leave little to no record, making it easier to deflect pushback and secure ambiguous agreements. This chapter explores how this tactic is used and how to recognize and counter it.

## 1. Securing Task Agreements Over Calls

Calls are often used to secure task agreements without leaving a paper trail. This approach can be especially effective for those looking to shift responsibilities subtly.

**Tactic 1: Ambiguous Agreement**

- **Description:** During a call, the person pushing the task secures a vague agreement from the other party without clear details.
- **Example:** "Can you handle this for me?" followed by a non-specific affirmation like "Sure, I'll look into it."
- **Impact:** The lack of detail means the person agreeing can later claim they didn't fully understand the scope, while the task initiator can assert that an agreement was made.

**Tactic 2: Rapid Task Assignment**

- **Description:** Quickly assigning tasks during a call to minimize the other party's opportunity to decline or ask questions.

- **Example:** "I need you to take care of this by tomorrow. Thanks!" before quickly moving to the next topic.
- **Impact:** The rushed nature of the request can lead to an unintentional agreement, with the other party feeling pressured to comply.

**Tactic 3: Friendly Pressure**

- **Description:** Using a friendly tone to secure task agreements, making it harder for the other party to refuse.
- **Example:** "Hey, buddy, can you do this little favor for me? It won't take long."
- **Impact:** The informal, friendly approach reduces resistance, as people are generally more inclined to help friends or colleagues they get along with.

**Tactic 4: Assumptive Close**

- **Description:** Speaking as if the agreement is already in place, prompting the other party to agree by default.
- **Example:** "So, you'll handle that report for the meeting, right?" spoken as a statement rather than a question.
- **Impact:** The assumption embedded in the statement often leads to compliance, as it implies the decision has already been made.

**2. Deflecting Pushback During Calls**

When pushback occurs, skilled manipulators use various techniques to deflect it and reinforce the initial agreement.

**Strategy 1: Reframing the Task**

- **Description:** Reframing the task as something manageable or beneficial to the person being asked.
- **Example:** "I know it's a bit extra, but it'll be great for your portfolio."
- **Impact:** Reframing can reduce resistance by making the task seem more appealing or less burdensome.

## Strategy 2: Leveraging Urgency

- **Description:** Emphasizing the urgency of the task to minimize objections.
- **Example:** "We need this done ASAP; it's critical for the project's success."
- **Impact:** Urgency creates a sense of immediate need, compelling the other person to agree despite reservations.

## Strategy 3: Creating Dependency

- **Description:** Making the task seem essential for the requester's work to proceed, implying a dependency.
- **Example:** "I can't move forward without your input on this."
- **Impact:** This creates a sense of responsibility and importance, making it harder for the person to refuse.

## Strategy 4: Deferring Detailed Questions

- **Description:** Deflecting detailed questions about the task by promising to send more information later.
- **Example:** "Great question! I'll send you all the details in an email after this call."
- **Impact:** This tactic temporarily satisfies the other party, securing their agreement before they fully understand the scope.

## Practical Examples

## Example 1: Ambiguous Agreement

- **Scenario:** A team leader securing task acceptance during a call.
- **Execution:** "Can you handle this for me?" and receiving a vague "Sure, I'll look into it."
- **Impact:** Leaves room for later disputes about the task's specifics, but the leader can claim agreement.

### Example 2: Rapid Task Assignment

- **Scenario:** A manager assigning tasks quickly during a status update call.
- **Execution:** "I need this by end of day, thanks!" followed by an immediate topic change.
- **Impact:** The abrupt request leaves the subordinate little room to refuse.

### Example 3: Friendly Pressure

- **Scenario:** A colleague asking for help in a casual call.
- **Execution:** "Hey, can you cover this for me? It's just a small thing."
- **Impact:** The friendly tone makes it hard to refuse without seeming uncooperative.

### Example 4: Assumptive Close

- **Scenario:** A project manager concluding a task assignment.
- **Execution:** "You'll handle the client meeting prep, right?" spoken as a given.
- **Impact:** The implied agreement often results in compliance.

### Example 5: Reframing the Task

- **Scenario:** A team lead asking for extra work.
- **Execution:** "It'll look great on your annual review."
- **Impact:** Makes the task seem beneficial, reducing resistance.

### Example 6: Leveraging Urgency

- **Scenario:** A supervisor needing immediate assistance.
- **Execution:** "This needs to be done today, or the project will be delayed."
- **Impact:** The urgency prompts quick compliance.

### Example 7: Creating Dependency

- **Scenario:** A project manager explaining task importance.
- **Execution:** "I can't finalize the report without your figures."
- **Impact:** Implies the other person's input is crucial, prompting agreement.

### Example 8: Deferring Detailed Questions

- **Scenario:** A colleague deflecting questions during a call.
- **Execution:** "I'll send you all the details in an email."
- **Impact:** Temporarily satisfies the person, securing agreement first.

### Conclusion

Securing agreements by call is a tactic that relies on the absence of a written record and the immediacy of verbal communication. By understanding how ambiguous agreements, rapid task assignments, friendly pressure, and assumptive closes work, you can better navigate these situations. Recognize these tactics and respond with clarity and requests for written follow-ups to ensure accountability and prevent unfair burden. This chapter provides insights into maintaining transparency and fair responsibility distribution in the workplace.

# CHAPTER 24: ASSIGNING UNRELATED TASKS

In the workplace, assigning unrelated tasks is a common tactic used to push work, blame, or responsibility onto others. This chapter explores how tasks that aren't directly related to one's role are assigned, and how to recognize and counter these tactics effectively.

## 1. Indirectly Assigning Tasks

Indirect task assignment is a subtle way of offloading work without explicitly stating it. This method leverages ambiguity and implied responsibility to shift tasks to others.

**Tactic 1: Implicit Requests**

- **Description:** Making indirect suggestions or comments that imply the need for action without directly assigning the task.
- **Example:** "It would be great if someone could look into this issue."
- **Impact:** The ambiguity of the request makes it difficult for others to refuse, as it appears to be a collective responsibility.

**Tactic 2: Highlighting Gaps**

- **Description:** Pointing out gaps or issues that need addressing, subtly implying that someone should take it upon themselves to handle it.

- **Example:** "We seem to be missing some data on this report. Can anyone help fill in the details?"
- **Impact:** This approach subtly pressures team members to step in and take responsibility.

**Tactic 3: Suggesting Improvements**

- **Description:** Offering suggestions for improvements or changes that implicitly require someone else to implement them.
- **Example:** "Our current process could be more efficient if we tracked our metrics more closely."
- **Impact:** Team members may feel compelled to take on the task of implementing these suggestions to demonstrate initiative.

**Tactic 4: General Assignments in Meetings**

- **Description:** Assigning tasks during meetings in a general manner, without specifying who is responsible.
- **Example:** "We need to get this done by next week. Let's make sure it happens."
- **Impact:** This leaves the responsibility open-ended, with the expectation that someone will step up.

## 2. Execution of Passing on Responsibilities

Once tasks are indirectly assigned, the execution phase involves reinforcing the assignment and ensuring the responsibility is accepted by someone else.

**Strategy 1: Follow-Up Questions**

- **Description:** Asking follow-up questions that reinforce the task assignment without explicitly stating it.
- **Example:** "Have we made any progress on that issue?" directed at the group.
- **Impact:** This reinforces the expectation that someone should have taken responsibility.

**Strategy 2: Positive Reinforcement**

- **Description:** Praising individuals who take on the task, encouraging others to follow suit in the future.
- **Example:** "Great job on handling that last-minute request, John!"
- **Impact:** Positive reinforcement creates a culture where taking on additional tasks is seen as commendable.

## Strategy 3: Silent Approval

- **Description:** Allowing tasks to be taken on without explicit approval, thereby endorsing the action passively.
- **Example:** When someone starts working on the task, the manager does not intervene or redistribute it.
- **Impact:** The lack of intervention implies acceptance and endorsement of the task assignment.

## Strategy 4: Task Expansion

- **Description:** Expanding the scope of a task subtly to include additional responsibilities.
- **Example:** "While you're working on that report, could you also look into our quarterly figures?"
- **Impact:** This increases the burden on the person who has already taken on the initial task.

## Practical Examples

## Example 1: Implicit Requests

- **Scenario:** A manager suggesting improvements during a team meeting.
- **Execution:** "It would be great if someone could streamline our onboarding process."
- **Impact:** Team members may feel compelled to take on the task voluntarily.

## Example 2: Highlighting Gaps

- **Scenario:** A team leader pointing out missing data in a

project.
- **Execution:** "We seem to be missing some key metrics here. Can anyone assist?"
- **Impact:** Subtle pressure on team members to step in and address the issue.

**Example 3: Suggesting Improvements**
- **Scenario:** A supervisor suggesting process improvements.
- **Execution:** "We could really benefit from a better inventory tracking system."
- **Impact:** Team members may feel the need to take initiative and implement changes.

**Example 4: General Assignments in Meetings**
- **Scenario:** A project manager giving general task assignments.
- **Execution:** "Let's ensure this project is completed by next Friday."
- **Impact:** Leaves the responsibility open-ended, expecting team members to self-assign.

**Example 5: Follow-Up Questions**
- **Scenario:** A manager checking on progress indirectly.
- **Execution:** "Has anyone started working on the new client proposal?"
- **Impact:** Reinforces the expectation that someone should have taken responsibility.

**Example 6: Positive Reinforcement**
- **Scenario:** A team leader praising extra effort.
- **Execution:** "Thanks for stepping up and handling that task, Sarah!"
- **Impact:** Encourages others to take on additional tasks for recognition.

### Example 7: Silent Approval

- **Scenario:** A supervisor allowing task ownership to remain unchallenged.
- **Execution:** When a team member begins working on an extra task, the supervisor does not intervene.
- **Impact:** Implies acceptance and approval of the task assignment.

### Example 8: Task Expansion

- **Scenario:** A project lead expanding the scope of a task.
- **Execution:** "While you're updating the database, could you also check the data accuracy?"
- **Impact:** Increases the burden on the person handling the initial task.

### Conclusion

Assigning unrelated tasks is a subtle but effective way to shift work, blame, or responsibility onto others. By understanding the tactics of implicit requests, highlighting gaps, suggesting improvements, and making general assignments, you can better navigate these situations. Recognize these tactics and respond with clarity and assertiveness to ensure fair task distribution and accountability. This chapter provides insights into maintaining a balanced workload and preventing the unfair shifting of responsibilities in the workplace.

# CHAPTER 25: SALES DYNAMICS

Sales dynamics in the workplace often involve balancing the efforts of closing deals with supporting tasks that ensure smooth operations. This chapter delves into the tactics used to push work, blame, or responsibility within sales teams and how to navigate these complexities effectively.

## 1. Balancing Sales Efforts with Support Tasks

Sales teams frequently face the challenge of balancing their primary objective—closing deals—with numerous support tasks. These tasks can range from administrative duties to providing detailed information to internal teams.

### Tactic 1: Overloading New Sales Staff

- **Description:** Assigning additional support tasks to new sales staff under the guise of helping them learn the ropes.
- **Example:** "Since you're new, it would be good for you to handle these reports to understand our process better."
- **Impact:** New staff may feel overwhelmed and unable to focus on their primary sales responsibilities.

### Tactic 2: Splitting Sales and Support Roles

- **Description:** Implicitly assigning support tasks to certain members of the sales team while others focus solely on selling.
- **Example:** "Can you handle the customer follow-ups while I focus on closing this new deal?"

- **Impact:** Creates an imbalance in workload and can lead to resentment among team members.

**Tactic 3: Using Administrative Tasks as Training**

- **Description:** Framing administrative support tasks as a necessary part of sales training.
- **Example:** "Handling these data entries will give you a better understanding of our sales metrics."
- **Impact:** Diverts time and energy away from actual selling activities.

**Tactic 4: Delegating Customer Queries**

- **Description:** Assigning customer queries and follow-ups to less experienced sales staff.
- **Example:** "Can you follow up with this customer while I work on a new prospect?"
- **Impact:** Shifts the burden of maintaining customer relationships to less experienced team members.

## 2. Methods for Ensuring End-to-End Responsibility

Ensuring end-to-end responsibility in sales means that salespeople must not only close deals but also ensure the seamless execution of related tasks. This section explores tactics that push full responsibility onto sales staff, often leading to increased pressure and potential burnout.

**Strategy 1: Full Accountability for Deals**

- **Description:** Making sales staff responsible for every aspect of the sales process, from initial contact to post-sale support.
- **Example:** "You're responsible for this client from start to finish, including any issues that arise post-sale."
- **Impact:** Increases workload and stress on sales staff, as they must manage multiple aspects of the process.

**Strategy 2: End-to-End Documentation**

- **Description:** Requiring detailed documentation and

follow-ups for each sale.
- **Example:** "Make sure you document every step of the process and follow up with the client regularly."
- **Impact:** Adds administrative burden to sales roles, reducing time available for pursuing new leads.

**Strategy 3: Involving Sales in Implementation**
- **Description:** Making salespeople responsible for the implementation of the solutions they sell.
- **Example:** "After closing the deal, you need to coordinate with the technical team to ensure proper implementation."
- **Impact:** Sales staff must take on additional coordination roles, diverting focus from selling.

**Strategy 4: Customer Handholding**
- **Description:** Requiring sales staff to guide customers through every step of the buying process.
- **Example:** "You need to be available for the customer at every stage to answer any questions they might have."
- **Impact:** Increases the time and effort required from sales staff, leading to potential inefficiencies.

**Practical Examples**

**Example 1: Overloading New Sales Staff**
- **Scenario:** A new sales employee being assigned multiple support tasks.
- **Execution:** "To help you get up to speed, handle these client follow-ups and report back."
- **Impact:** The new employee feels overwhelmed and struggles to balance learning and selling.

**Example 2: Splitting Sales and Support Roles**
- **Scenario:** A senior sales rep delegating support tasks to a junior team member.

- **Execution:** "You handle the CRM updates while I focus on this new client."
- **Impact:** The junior team member ends up with a disproportionate workload.

**Example 3: Using Administrative Tasks as Training**

- **Scenario:** New sales staff assigned data entry as part of their training.
- **Execution:** "Entering these figures will help you understand our sales pipeline better."
- **Impact:** Diverts time from actual sales activities to administrative tasks.

**Example 4: Delegating Customer Queries**

- **Scenario:** A senior salesperson pushing customer follow-ups to a less experienced colleague.
- **Execution:** "Can you follow up with the client about their latest order?"
- **Impact:** Increases workload on less experienced staff, potentially affecting their performance.

**Example 5: Full Accountability for Deals**

- **Scenario:** A salesperson responsible for all aspects of the sale.
- **Execution:** "Ensure you handle everything from initial contact to after-sale support."
- **Impact:** Increases pressure and workload on the salesperson, leading to potential burnout.

**Example 6: End-to-End Documentation**

- **Scenario:** A sales rep required to document every step of the sales process.
- **Execution:** "Document each interaction and follow up with detailed notes."
- **Impact:** Adds administrative tasks, reducing time for

selling.

## Example 7: Involving Sales in Implementation

- **Scenario:** Sales staff coordinating implementation post-sale.
- **Execution:** "Coordinate with the technical team to ensure the solution is implemented correctly."
- **Impact:** Diverts focus from selling to managing implementation.

## Example 8: Customer Handholding

- **Scenario:** A salesperson required to guide the customer through every stage.
- **Execution:** "Be available to answer any customer questions throughout the process."
- **Impact:** Increases time commitment and reduces efficiency.

## Conclusion

Balancing sales efforts with support tasks and ensuring end-to-end responsibility can lead to increased workloads and stress for sales teams. By recognizing these tactics, sales staff can better navigate their responsibilities and advocate for a more balanced distribution of tasks. Understanding how to handle overloading, splitting roles, using administrative tasks as training, and other common tactics will help create a more equitable and efficient work environment.

# CHAPTER 26: CONSTRAINTS MANAGEMENT

Constraints management is an essential aspect of workplace dynamics, often involving the identification and handling of limitations that affect productivity and efficiency. This chapter explores how individuals in the workplace use tactics to push the responsibility of managing constraints onto others, thereby alleviating their own burden.

### 1. Delegating Constraints Management

Delegating constraints management involves shifting the responsibility of identifying and resolving limitations to others, often under the guise of collaboration or team effort. This tactic allows individuals to appear proactive while actually avoiding the work themselves.

**Tactic 1: Assigning Constraint Analysis**

- **Description:** Delegating the task of analyzing and identifying constraints to team members.
- **Example:** "Can you look into what might be causing these delays and come up with some solutions?"
- **Impact:** Shifts the burden of constraint identification to others, saving time and effort for the delegator.

**Tactic 2: Requesting Regular Updates**

- **Description:** Asking for regular updates on constraints without directly contributing to their resolution.

- **Example:** "I need a weekly report on the bottlenecks we're facing in this project."
- **Impact:** Places the responsibility of monitoring and reporting constraints on others.

**Tactic 3: Forming Committees**

- **Description:** Creating committees or task forces to handle constraints, often with minimal involvement from the initiator.
- **Example:** "Let's form a team to address these resource limitations."
- **Impact:** Distributes the workload among multiple people, reducing the initiator's involvement.

**Tactic 4: Pushing Constraints as Learning Opportunities**

- **Description:** Framing the management of constraints as a learning opportunity for less experienced staff.
- **Example:** "Handling this budget constraint will be a great learning experience for you."
- **Impact:** Delegates difficult tasks to less experienced team members under the pretense of professional development.

### 2. Practical Examples of Pushing Constraints

Practical examples of pushing constraints involve real-world scenarios where individuals avoid dealing with limitations by passing the responsibility to others.

**Example 1: Assigning Constraint Analysis**

- **Scenario:** A project manager faces delays in project timelines.
- **Execution:** "I need you to analyze the delays and propose solutions by the end of the week."
- **Impact:** The team member spends time identifying and resolving issues, freeing the manager from this task.

**Example 2: Requesting Regular Updates**

- **Scenario:** A department head wants to keep track of resource limitations.
- **Execution:** "Please provide me with a weekly update on our resource utilization and any constraints."
- **Impact:** The team members compile and report the data, while the department head reviews it without contributing to the resolution.

### Example 3: Forming Committees

- **Scenario:** A senior executive identifies multiple operational bottlenecks.
- **Execution:** "Let's create a committee to address these bottlenecks and improve our processes."
- **Impact:** The committee members handle the detailed work, while the executive remains relatively hands-off.

### Example 4: Pushing Constraints as Learning Opportunities

- **Scenario:** A team leader identifies a significant budget constraint in a project.
- **Execution:** "This budget issue is complex, but resolving it will be a valuable experience for you."
- **Impact:** The less experienced team member tackles the budget constraint, gaining experience while the leader avoids direct involvement.

### Example 5: Using Collaborative Tools

- **Scenario:** A product manager faces limitations in development resources.
- **Execution:** "Let's use our project management software to track and address these resource issues."
- **Impact:** Team members use the software to identify and manage constraints, reducing the manager's hands-on involvement.

### Example 6: Leveraging External Consultants

- **Scenario:** A company encounters regulatory constraints in a new market.
- **Execution:** "We'll hire a consulting firm to navigate these regulatory issues for us."
- **Impact:** The consulting firm handles the constraints, allowing the company to focus on other areas.

## Conclusion

Delegating constraints management is a common tactic used to push the responsibility of handling limitations onto others. By understanding these tactics, employees can better navigate their roles and advocate for fairer distribution of workload. Recognizing how constraints are pushed as learning opportunities, through regular updates, committee formations, or by leveraging external resources, helps create a more balanced and efficient work environment. This awareness allows employees to address constraints collaboratively while ensuring that no single individual bears the brunt of the workload unfairly.

# CHAPTER 27: ADAPTIVE COMMUNICATION

Adaptive communication involves the ability to flip one's words or stance according to the situation. This tactic can be used to navigate complex workplace dynamics, deflect responsibility, or shift blame. In this chapter, we will explore how individuals use adaptive communication to their advantage and the techniques for situational responses.

## 1. Flipping Words as the Situation Requires

Flipping words or changing one's stance as the situation demands is a tactic used to maintain a favorable position, avoid accountability, or manipulate the narrative.

### Tactic 1: Changing Stance Based on Feedback

- **Description:** Adapting one's opinion or statement based on the feedback received.
- **Example:** Initially supporting a project proposal but changing stance if the higher-ups criticize it. "I always had reservations about this plan; we should consider alternative approaches."
- **Impact:** This flexibility allows the individual to align with the prevailing sentiment, avoiding conflict or responsibility.

### Tactic 2: Ambiguous Statements

- **Description:** Making statements that can be interpreted in multiple ways, allowing for flexibility in future discussions.

- **Example:** "We should consider all options moving forward." This can later be clarified to support or oppose specific actions as needed.
- **Impact:** Ambiguity provides a safety net, allowing the individual to adapt their stance based on future developments.

**Tactic 3: Selective Memory**

- **Description:** Claiming to remember or forget details selectively to suit the situation.
- **Example:** "I don't recall agreeing to that specific deadline." This can be used to avoid blame or responsibility for unmet commitments.
- **Impact:** Selective memory can deflect criticism and create room for renegotiation of terms or responsibilities.

## 2. Techniques for Situational Responses

Situational responses involve adapting communication strategies based on the immediate context and the audience's reaction. Here are some techniques for effective situational responses:

**Technique 1: Reading the Room**

- **Description:** Assessing the mood, opinions, and reactions of the audience before responding.
- **Example:** Observing body language and tone during a meeting to gauge support or opposition before making a statement.
- **Impact:** This technique ensures that responses are aligned with the audience's sentiment, reducing the risk of conflict.

**Technique 2: Rephrasing for Clarity or Ambiguity**

- **Description:** Rephrasing statements to either clarify or introduce ambiguity based on the situation.

- **Example:** "What I meant to say was..." can be used to clarify a position if challenged, or "Let's leave our options open" can introduce ambiguity.
- **Impact:** Rephrasing can help manage misunderstandings and provide flexibility for future discussions.

## Technique 3: Deflecting with Questions

- **Description:** Responding to inquiries with questions to redirect focus or clarify the asker's intent.
- **Example:** "Can you elaborate on what you mean by that?" or "What are your thoughts on this issue?"
- **Impact:** This technique buys time, clarifies the situation, and can shift the burden of explanation back to the questioner.

## Technique 4: Agreeing Generally, Opposing Specifically

- **Description:** Agreeing with general principles while opposing specific implementations.
- **Example:** "I agree that efficiency is important, but I have concerns about this particular method."
- **Impact:** This allows the individual to appear cooperative while maintaining opposition to specific points.

## Technique 5: Utilizing Diplomatic Language

- **Description:** Using neutral or positive language to defuse tension and maintain flexibility.
- **Example:** "Let's explore this further before making a decision." or "I see your point, let's consider all perspectives."
- **Impact:** Diplomatic language helps maintain a collaborative atmosphere and leaves room for maneuvering.

## Technique 6: Playing the Devil's Advocate

- **Description:** Positioning oneself as exploring all options by presenting counterarguments.
- **Example:** "Just to play devil's advocate, have we considered the potential downsides?"
- **Impact:** This technique allows the individual to present opposing views without committing to them.

## Conclusion

Adaptive communication, or "prata," is a powerful tactic in workplace dynamics. By flipping words as the situation requires and using situational response techniques, individuals can navigate complex interactions, avoid blame, and shift responsibilities. Understanding these tactics helps employees recognize when they are being used and develop strategies to respond effectively, ensuring fairer and more transparent communication in the workplace.

# CHAPTER 28: FAMILY-RUN BUSINESSES

Family-run businesses come with their unique set of dynamics and challenges. Navigating these environments requires an understanding of the internal politics and strategies for avoiding pitfalls or adapting effectively. In this chapter, we will explore the intricacies of family-run businesses and offer practical advice for thriving within them.

## 1. Navigating Internal Politics

Internal politics in family-run businesses can be particularly intricate due to the overlapping of personal relationships and professional roles. Understanding these dynamics is crucial for anyone working in such an environment.

**Understanding Family Hierarchies**

- **Description:** Recognizing the family hierarchy and power structures within the business.
- **Example:** Being aware of who holds the decision-making power and who influences them.
- **Impact:** This awareness helps in navigating the decision-making process and aligning oneself with key influencers.

**Respecting Established Relationships**

- **Description:** Acknowledging and respecting the long-standing relationships and loyalties within the family.
- **Example:** Avoiding actions that could be perceived as undermining these relationships.

- **Impact:** Respecting these dynamics can prevent conflicts and help in gaining trust and support.

### Managing Favoritism

- **Description:** Dealing with favoritism, where family members or close associates may receive preferential treatment.
- **Example:** Focusing on building merit-based achievements and demonstrating value to the business.
- **Impact:** Highlighting one's contributions and achievements can help in gaining recognition despite favoritism.

### Recognizing Informal Channels of Communication

- **Description:** Understanding that informal communication channels often play a significant role in family-run businesses.
- **Example:** Engaging in casual conversations and gatherings to stay informed and build relationships.
- **Impact:** Leveraging these channels can provide valuable insights and strengthen one's position within the company.

## 2. Strategies for Avoidance and Adaptation

While navigating the complexities of a family-run business, certain strategies can help avoid common pitfalls and adapt effectively to the environment.

### Establishing Clear Boundaries

- **Description:** Setting clear boundaries between personal and professional interactions.
- **Example:** Keeping discussions professional during work hours and avoiding getting involved in family disputes.
- **Impact:** Clear boundaries help maintain professionalism and reduce the risk of being drawn into family conflicts.

## Building Alliances with Non-Family Members

- **Description:** Forming alliances with other non-family employees who share similar experiences and challenges.
- **Example:** Collaborating on projects and supporting each other in navigating the family dynamics.
- **Impact:** These alliances can provide a support system and collective strength to address common issues.

## Demonstrating Neutrality

- **Description:** Maintaining a neutral stance in family conflicts and disputes.
- **Example:** Avoiding taking sides and focusing on work-related matters.
- **Impact:** Neutrality helps in maintaining professional relationships and avoiding backlash from any family faction.

## Adapting to Cultural Norms

- **Description:** Understanding and adapting to the cultural norms and values of the family.
- **Example:** Observing how decisions are made, how respect is shown, and how conflicts are resolved.
- **Impact:** Adapting to these norms helps in fitting into the company culture and gaining acceptance.

## Effective Communication

- **Description:** Communicating effectively to navigate misunderstandings and clarify expectations.
- **Example:** Being clear and concise in communication, and confirming understanding through follow-ups.
- **Impact:** Effective communication can prevent misinterpretations and ensure smooth collaboration.

## Seeking Mentorship and Guidance

- **Description:** Finding a mentor within or outside the family who understands the dynamics and can offer guidance.
- **Example:** Seeking advice on navigating tricky situations and making strategic career moves.
- **Impact:** A mentor can provide valuable insights and support in navigating the unique challenges of a family-run business.

## Conclusion

Working in a family-run business presents unique challenges and opportunities. By understanding the internal politics and implementing strategies for avoidance and adaptation, employees can navigate these environments more effectively. Building alliances, maintaining neutrality, and communicating clearly are key tactics for thriving in a family-run business. Recognizing and respecting the family dynamics while focusing on one's professional contributions can lead to a more rewarding and successful career within such an organization.

# CONCLUSION

In this book, we have explored various tactics used by difficult bosses and colleagues to push work, blame, and responsibility onto others. These strategies, while often detrimental to a healthy work environment, are prevalent in many workplaces. Understanding these tactics and learning how to navigate them is crucial for maintaining your productivity, morale, and professional reputation. In this conclusion, we will recap the strategies discussed and provide some final thoughts on workplace dynamics.

## 1. Recap of Strategies

Throughout the chapters, we covered a wide array of tactics employed by challenging individuals in the workplace. Here is a summary of the key strategies discussed:

**Improving Productivity by Redistribution**

- Tactic: Taking work from one person or department and pushing it to others.
- Strategy: Recognize and mitigate attempts to offload tasks unfairly.

**The "I Don't Know" Mindset**

- Tactic: Claiming ignorance to avoid responsibility.
- Strategy: Document interactions and maintain clear records of task assignments.

**The "Already Told You" Tactic**

- Tactic: Providing minimal information and claiming prior communication.
- Strategy: Request detailed clarifications and confirm

understandings in writing.

**Feigning Ignorance**

- Tactic: Pretending not to understand to frustrate others into doing the work.
- Strategy: Be patient and persistent in requiring contributions and accountability.

**The "My Job is Done" Approach**

- Tactic: Completing tasks superficially and transferring responsibility for review.
- Strategy: Set clear expectations for thoroughness and hold individuals accountable for their work.

**Countering by Asking**

- Tactic: Deflecting questions back to the requestor to avoid providing answers.
- Strategy: Insist on direct responses and provide necessary guidance.

**Selective Hearing**

- Tactic: Ignoring unwanted input.
- Strategy: Address ignored points directly and seek acknowledgment.

**Keeping Things Vocal**

- Tactic: Relying on oral communication to avoid accountability.
- Strategy: Insist on written records and documented agreements.

**Saying You Understand**

- Tactic: Claiming understanding publicly, seeking clarification privately.
- Strategy: Confirm understanding and action items during meetings.

**The Power of Assumptions**

- Tactic: Using assumptions to shift responsibility.
- Strategy: Clarify roles and responsibilities explicitly.

**Strategic Silence**

- Tactic: Staying silent in meetings to avoid responsibility.
- Strategy: Engage proactively and seek contributions from silent participants.

**The Call Strategy**

- Tactic: Avoiding written communication by suggesting calls.
- Strategy: Document call discussions and follow up with written summaries.

**Testing Market Reactions**

- Tactic: Using humor to gauge reactions and test boundaries.
- Strategy: Respond appropriately to maintain professional boundaries.

**Hidden Responsibilities**

- Tactic: Assigning tasks indirectly during meetings.
- Strategy: Clarify and document all assigned tasks and responsibilities.

**Using Higher Authority**

- Tactic: Leveraging authority figures to assign tasks.
- Strategy: Verify the legitimacy of authority-based requests.

**Generic Agreements**

- Tactic: Securing broad approvals to cover various scenarios.
- Strategy: Seek detailed explanations and context for all agreements.

**Passing Responsibility**

- Tactic: Shifting blame and responsibility to others.
- Strategy: Hold individuals accountable and confirm their commitments.

**New Boss Dynamics**

- Tactic: Redistributing tasks to a new boss.
- Strategy: Clearly define and communicate roles and expectations with new leadership.

**Saying No**

- Tactic: Refusing tasks without offering alternatives.
- Strategy: Encourage collaborative problem-solving and suggest viable solutions.

**Teamwork Rhetoric**

- Tactic: Using teamwork language to transition responsibility.
- Strategy: Clearly delineate individual contributions and follow up on commitments.

**Minimal Email Communication**

- Tactic: Sending concise emails to delegate tasks.
- Strategy: Request detailed information and confirm responsibilities in follow-ups.

**Misleading Through Silence**

- Tactic: Using non-verbal cues to imply task ownership.
- Strategy: Address ambiguities directly and confirm task ownership explicitly.

**Agreement by Call**

- Tactic: Securing task agreements over calls and deflecting pushback.
- Strategy: Document call agreements and address pushback promptly.

**Assigning Unrelated Tasks**

- Tactic: Assigning tasks indirectly related to agreed-upon responsibilities.
- Strategy: Confirm task scope and relevance before agreeing to take on work.

**Sales Dynamics**

- Tactic: Balancing sales efforts with support tasks.
- Strategy: Ensure clear boundaries between sales and support responsibilities.

**Constraints Management**

- Tactic: Delegating constraints management to others.
- Strategy: Define and communicate constraints clearly and equitably.

**Adaptive Communication (Prata)**

- Tactic: Flipping words as the situation requires.
- Strategy: Maintain consistency and transparency in communication.

**Family-Run Businesses**

- Tactic: Navigating internal politics in family-run businesses.
- Strategy: Respect family dynamics, build alliances, and maintain professionalism.

## 2. Final Thoughts on Workplace Dynamics

Navigating the complex dynamics of a workplace filled with challenging personalities requires a combination of awareness, strategic thinking, and resilience. By understanding the tactics used by difficult bosses and colleagues, you can better protect yourself from being unfairly burdened with additional work, blame, or responsibility.

It's essential to foster a workplace culture that values clear communication, accountability, and mutual respect. Encourage transparency and collaboration, and strive to lead by example. When faced with manipulative tactics, remain calm and focused on your goals, using the strategies outlined in this book to navigate and counter these challenges effectively.

Ultimately, maintaining your integrity and professionalism is paramount. While it may be tempting to adopt similar tactics in response, it's important to uphold your ethical standards and contribute to a positive work environment. By doing so, you not only protect your own reputation but also inspire others to follow suit, leading to a more productive and harmonious workplace for everyone.

www.ingramcontent.com/pod-product-compliance
Lightning Source LLC
Chambersburg PA
CBHW071931210526
45479CB00002B/636